This Way is my Way

Russell Street Memories

(a sentimental journey home)

RICHARD TODD CANTON

iUniverse, Inc.
New York   Bloomington

iUniverse books may be ordered through booksellers or by contacting:

iUniverse
1663 Liberty Drive
Bloomington, IN 47403
www.iuniverse.com
1-800-Authors (1-800-288-4677)

Because of the dynamic nature of the Internet, any Web addresses or links contained in this book may have changed since publication and may no longer be valid. The views expressed in this work are solely those of the author and do not necessarily reflect the views of the publisher, and the publisher hereby disclaims any responsibility for them.

ISBN: 978-1-4502-4651-4 (sc)
ISBN: 978-1-4502-4652-1 (ebook)

Printed in the United States of America

iUniverse rev. date: 09/23/2010

Preface

Within the covers of this book lie the stories of a young boy's coming of age. Growing up is not that easy for anyone, particularly a fatherless boy who is clumsy, inept and not very talented. It was his mother who first saw potential in him and through her encouragement and relentless drive, made a man out of him. I am that boy and these stories all have one thing in common, my love for family and friends and a true sense of the value of life and love. Vivian Gillis is my mother and I am your host, Todd Canton.

It was upon the rude awakening of my father's death that I first took notice of my mother. There she stood at 43 years of age, overweight and slovenly. Our father had always been so immaculate about himself, but our mother seemed to let herself go. Perhaps it was because she had so many children to take care of, or even that her marriage had soured, who knows? Whatever it was that was going on with her personally at the time, was immensely overshadowed by the fact that her husband was dead, and she was left with a pile of children to raise. A financially strapped future faced us all. She, being of sound mind and body took on the task at hand, putting her family and it's needs first, quite often doing without for herself. Vivian Gillis, these are her stories........

COAL

When a young Vivian Gillis left the town of Springhill, Nova Scotia in 1948 to be married, she so looked forward to her life, yet longed for home. The close knit ties of a coal mining family are carefully interwoven and uneasy to sever, perhaps due to a lot of pain and anguish. The kind of pain and anguish that goes along with the tragedies afforded coal mining families.

The depth and darkness of the Cumberland mine has been described over and over as the blackest of black, the loneliest of lonely and the coldest of cold. But it is with those above ground that the worry sets in and the waiting takes place. Everyday the miners dig a little deeper , miles beneath the earth's crust.

Vivian Gillis's father Dan and his brothers were all the men of the deep mines. All bore the scars of this difficult and weary life. Most of them aged before their time, suffered illness later in life but coal mining was in their blood. A hard old life for these resilient and valiant men. As Vivian Gillis and her husband Bert were in the process of creating a family Amherst, tragedy struck. Fully pregnant with her fourth child the news came from Springhill. November 1956, a devastating mine explosion. Vivian Gillis, beside herself with grief, waited for her husband to come home and safely deliver her to her family.

The drive from Amherst to Springhill is a beautiful one at the best of times but in the fall is it is just short of spectacular. The color of the leaves , the ones that hadn't fallen, were able to channel her thoughts back to her childhood and the many strolls she would take through the untouched forest. The sound of the sirens broke her concentration and brought her back to reality. As they got closer and closer to the town the traffic thickened. Cars, trucks, police, fire engines, ambulances. Dense smoke hung in the air and the stench of death was all about. This dreary vision of Springhill is one that Vivian Gillis would hold in her soul forever. Tragedy brings people out in the streets. All met near the face of the mine. Doctors, miners, draegermen, business men and the intense and profound sound of crying. Just as they were able to bring some to the surface word came that friends and family alike had lost someone dear.

A cousin, an uncle, a friend, lost Such is the life of a miner's family. Blood and bone is the price for coal, pain and suffering linger in your soul. Vivian Gillis, like every other true Springhiller took the disaster in stride. She supported those who needed it, fed the families of the miners, opened her family home to those who needed a hot cup of tea or a place to lie down. The media swarmed the town, support came from all over the world, and as families came together to say goodbye to the lost ones, Vivian Gillis went home to Amherst to have her baby. Naturally upset by all that went on, Vivian suffered complications that sent her to the doctor. Blood pressure at an alarming rate might very well cause the death of her baby or even take her own life. So, she had to settle herself down. She did, and a few weeks later she held a baby girl in her arms.

As life moved forward Vivian and Bert and their four children lived a moderately quiet life. It was probably not their intention to have any more children but a couple of years later there she was, full with child, 1958, when the underground bump shook the town of Springhill nearly upside down. This time 74 men were killed, the other 100 survived, some barely. Loved ones collected their beaten and broken and the whole town mourned the losses together. This time the results were devastating enough to make the decision to permanently close the mines.

When one thinks about the disasters that we , as a world community, have had to face, it might be true that it produces some of the strongest and most resilient people. I don't think anything compares to the souls of the families of coal miners. Work, blood, sweat, worry, tears, death and more tears. Despite the obvious dangers involved, their abounds among them a true sense of the value of life, laughter and love. Those brave hard working men like Dan Gillis, his brothers Angus and Hughie, and sisters Francess Gillis, and Mary Soppa were determined to secure a better life for their children, far from the darkness of the mines. Dan Gillis didn't want Vivian to be a miner's wife. To him, there had to be a better life outside the walls of Springhill and there was. I should know,

Vivian Gillis is my mother.

A Winter In Amherst

I can still hear my grandfather Fred Canton saying, "Kids today don't know what winter is."

Winter, ah, what fun when you're a kid. There's skating, sliding, coasting down the hills on your toboggan, and of course, hockey. Winter is not so much fun when you are older, mostly due to the fact that we, the people of today, are busier, we have less time to do the things we want to, and have so much more to worry about. We also don't want to bundle up like our mothers used to make us when we were going out the door. We now rely on the warmth of our vehicles and a ticking clock to get us where we are going.

Lately I dread winter because it slows me down. I hate driving on the highway because all I ever seem to hear is about accidents and tragedies that result because of slippery roads. So we, tend to take it easier during those winter months. Now with global warming and all that, we may or may not have any snow at all. When it does come however, it comes!

One winter in Amherst especially comes to mind. The winds that blow across the Tantramar Marshes bring with them a lot of snow and freezing winds, you know, real winter. We had suffered through a few days of snowfall, leaving Amherst in a real standstill. It took the plows days to get everyone dug out. When that was done the snow banks on the side of the road were so huge that you had to be warned by your mother *not to touch the telephone wires*, while walking to school. It's almost unbelievable today unless you think about White Juan. Kids today don't know what winter is.

In West Amherst there lies the Chignecto Bird Sanctuary, or as we called it, the GLEN. The Glen in it's own right is a very beautiful haven for water fowl. Lakes upon tree lined lakes of beautiful clean water and as I said, hundreds of species of birds flock there, making their homes, feeding on the water life in the lakes, and live a peaceful life under the watchful eye of man. In winter the lakes freeze and if it stayed something like twenty below for ten days, then it was safe to skate on. For me it was a little scary at first, because I could feel the ice cracking under my feet and of course, there were always horror stories about people falling through the ice. Who knows if they were true or not?

Anyway, tobogganing was my favorite thing to do, and the hills at the sanctuary were steep so with all that snow and such big hills , down we would go. Flying through the air at uncontrollable speeds made your heart race, your adrenalin kept you warm and the struggle of re-climbing the hills made you tired. Loads of fun. My friend Brian and I or my cousin Edward would quite often walk across the marsh, pulling behind us, our toboggans. My sister Ruth would quite often want to tag along but I didn't want her to because then I was responsible for her, and I'll tell you now, Mother held us responsible for each other. However, one day, we let her tag along. As we approached the hill I told her she was too little to slide down the hill on the back of our toboggan. She didn't like that. *Too bad,* I thought, because, only two on the toboggans at a time, three would not be safe. Well guess what, we did it. First Edward, then me, and then Ruth. As the three of us soared toward the unknown, down the cold and snowy hills at great speed we hit a bump with resounding consequences. I fell off and rolled down the hill, Edward went the distance, but Ruth literally flew through the air, landing face down in the snow with a thud, unconscious. I was sure she was dead. As I made my way down the slippery hill I approached her lifeless body, calling her name. Half crying, I knew this was all my fault and that's when Ruth pulled her snow covered and bloodied face up and shouted "Let's do it again!" I looked at Edward in disbelief and he at me.

We did it again!

And So it Goes

When I woke this morning it was to the warmth snuggling of my wife into my back, a dog at my feet and a cat on the pillow near my neck. The musical sound of rain on the roof was my symphony, life is good.

Our backyard garden has come alive in the rain almost overnight. This year we all welcome summer after a long and dreary winter. All of us take advantage of the sun when it's out and we are all better because of it. My dog frolics in the grass and there are so many smells to intake that it often leaves her in a state of euphoria. When she's happy, I am happy.

My dog Rozie has added so much to my life that I don't think I can adequately ever find the words to put on this page, but you know me, I try. I love her in a way that I never loved anyone and to a depth I never knew existed. Her loving me in return only adds to the invisible bond between us. I am wise enough to know that it won't last forever and that someday we will have to say goodbye to each other. That will certainly be a day in history for me. If I think about it I realize that I think I can handle it because I have been saying goodbye all my life. Who am I kidding? It will kill me.

My first realization that life would be trying was when, at the age of eleven, I witnessed my father's doctor, standing in our kitchen telling our mother that it was hopeless where our father was concerned. He tried not to but he couldn't help crying. He knew it wasn't fair for a woman in her forties to be left a widow and with so many kids too. There she stood, big and fat, a curler in the front of her hair, wondering what would happen next. Yet, as I have stated on several occasions, she was strong. Not one to give up, she marched forward. That was a lifetime ago.

When Mother took ill and it became apparent to us her children, that her time was near, each of us accepted and dealt with it in our own way. No one can tell a person how to grieve, it is something we do entirely on our own. When I finally realized that she really was gone, I looked inside myself to find the answers and there she was, in my heart and on my mind, for a lifetime. Today she sits in the pages of my stories and unknowingly touches the lives of people who read and experience them. Her life was a gift to me and one I cherish. I am sensible enough to appreciate all I have had and do have in my life. She taught me that.

She also taught me to see the beautiful side of life. So here goes. As Sherry and I were preparing breakfast this morning, we watched through our kitchen window, a flurry of pheasants make their way down the hill through our flowery garden to pick up what dropped from our bird feeder. Affectionately known as Harvey and the girls, this majestic and handsome bird keeps a watchful eye out while the three plain pea-hens enjoy a healthy breakfast of bird seed. This is a daily ritual and one that keeps us fascinated so I can only imagine what it does for our cat Chloe who sits in the window totally entranced by what she sees.

A warm breeze blows across the lawn bringing with it the smell of mayflowers that grow abundantly in the fields up behind our home. The sun is making it's way outside with a promise that there is always hope, and I know there is. And so it goes........

...............a little tired from working the busy weekend, I think I might take a nap in the sun room, my wife snuggling into my back, a dog at my feet and a cat on a pillow near my neck, all is well, life is good.

Once again, life is good and all my thoughts run home to you Mother, thanks.

Newsreel 1956 Explosion in the Springhill Mine

The 1956 Explosion occurred on November 1, 1956 when a mine train hauling a load of fine coal dust up to the surface of the 25-year old Number 4 colliery to remove it from the pithead encountered a heavy flow of ventilation air being forced down the shaft by fans on the surface. The flow of air disturbed the dust on the ascending train cars so that it spread throughout the air of the shafts of No. 4. Before the train reached the surface, several of the cars broke loose and ran back down the slope of No. 4, derailing along the way and hitting a power line, causing it to arc and ignite the coal dust at the 5500 foot level (below the surface).

The resulting explosion blew up the slope to the surface where the additional oxygen created a massive blast which leveled the bank head on the surface - where the coal is hauled out from the mine in an angled shaft into a vertical building (the coal is then dropped into railway cars). The majority of devastation occurred to the surface buildings but many miners were trapped in the shaft with the derailed train cars and fallen support timbers and other items damaged by the explosion.

In a show of heroics, Draegermen (rescue miners) and barefaced miners (no breathing equipment) entered the 6100 foot deep shaft of No. 4 to aid their co-workers. In total 88 miners were rescued and 39 were killed in the explosion. Media coverage of the 1956 explosion was largely overshadowed by the Soviet invasion of Hungary on October 24, 1956 however Canadian and local media did offer extensive coverage of the second Springhill mining disaster.

Following the rescue effort, No. 4 and the connecting No. 2 collieries were sealed for several months to deprive the fires of oxygen. Upon reopening, the bodies of miners who remained below the surface were recovered and the mine returned to operation.

Angus Gillis : A Coal Miner's Story

November 1, 1956. Springhill, Nova Scotia.

After supper, on a Thursday afternoon, like every other afternoon, seven year old Vivian Gillis stood on the doorstep of her friend's home breathing in the fresh Nova Scotia air. Despite Fall approaching it was a lovelier than usual day. Warm and beautiful. Like every other day she would wait for her friend Dorothy to put on her coat and the two of them would go outside to play. Just as Dorothy opened the door to greet her young friend, Vivian felt a rumbling beneath her feet.

For a second or two she felt almost weightless as the compression beneath the earth made it's way to the surface. Feeling this turbulence beneath her , Vivian instinctively knew something was wrong. Exactly what was occurring she did not know. Looking toward the mines just a few houses away she could not believe what she saw. What appeared like a mushroom cloud at the mouth of the mine, the smoke and steam rose quickly and brilliantly, almost knocking the girls to the ground. Standing at her kitchen window looking out, Vivian's mother Nora felt the same tremor her daughter did. Knowing full well the damage of a mine collapse or a bump can do her first thought was with her little girl.

The whole event was surreal to the young blonde girl. Hearing her name being hollered, she turned to see her panicked mother running toward her, seconds after the explosion in the mine, that turned Springhill nearly upside down. Frozen with fear, the little girl just stood motionless waiting for her mother to rescue her. As Nora Gillis made her way through the falling debris, burning pieces of tin were crashing to the ground all around her.

Taking the girl by the hand, she told her to hurry and the two of them ran down the road together. Nora knew there would be safety at her own mother's house. By this time everyone had come out into the street. Most of them were unsure of what had happened but a few men, especially those whose lives revolved around the mine, knew this meant serious trouble.

As the dense smell of smoke and ash filled the air, the picturesque town of Springhill was engulfed in a nasty blanket of toxic and lethal gas. Mothers rushed their children inside as the sirens were screaming loudly around them. Men were running down the street toward the mines to see who was alive and who was not. Immediately some miners emerged from within the smoke and debris and gave word that the boom came from collier #4. Men were dead and dying. The people of Springhill came together as one and without a whisper of doubt, began to work to save the men of the deep dark mines.

Never did it occur to Vivian Gillis that her father might be hurt or killed. He was her hero. Angus Gillis, at 52 years of age should have long retired from the mine but like all of the men at that time, it was his life's work. He set off for work that day just like every other, not realizing that the events that would follow would change his life forever. Dynamite had always made Angus nervous but it was one of many hazards he faced as a coal miner, just like breathing in the coal dust, the dangers involved with the train cars and with the picks and shovels. These were something he accepted in stride.

It is said that when one is directly involved in any kind of an explosion that the whole situation is so surreal that, quite often, their memory is erased. That's exactly what happened to Angus and the men who worked beside him. A warm tingly sensation trickled up his left arm and as he looked down toward his wrist, heard a small puffing sound and saw a bright flash of light. Within seconds, his body was airlifted, almost weightless and he floated head over heels through space. A few more seconds passed and he found himself lying face down in the rubble and dust. Black. Dark. Cold.

There were a few cries for help as Angus shook his head, he could clearly hear them. It became obvious that the mine had collapsed around him, leaving only a 3 foot tall crawl space. For a moment it occurred to him that his own death was near, after all they were as far down as one could go. Trapped in the mine, so many feet below the surface, he literally could not see his hand in front of his face. Was he blinded by the blast? He did not know for sure. This was the kind of darkness that he could only ever imagine. Covered in blood, dry from the dust, and aching and paining in his chest and back, there was little else he could do but lie there and call out to anyone who might hear a pipe with flowing moderately fresh air was his life line.

As a Catholic family, prayer played a big role in their lives, both above and below ground. As Vivian sat beside her mother at St John's Catholic Church praying for the safe return of her father and his friends, Angus's thoughts drifted toward God as well. He thought about the day he got married in 1937 and how he was able to look out into the faces of his family, especially his mother. He thought about his children's baptisms, walking Vivian to Sunday school, and his own parents Dan & Franny Gillis. He knew deep inside that God was even closer to him now more than ever. They all did. That's why the hymns were sung by the remaining miners. Sitting in their own excrement and slowly starving to death, the days crawled by. Would someone save them? Would they ever see the light of day again? Would ever stare into the face of his wife and daughter again? This prison of darkness and silence was his judge now. He remained quiet, exhausted from the whole ordeal, dozing in and out of consciousness. What was thought to a trickle of water on his hand tasted like blood. Life sustaining blood. We will wait.

For a few days Nora and Vivian stayed at Nanny Phalen's. Friends and relatives were constantly coming and going from house to house, dropping of and picking up supplies and thermoses and food for those who were diligently working on the rescue of the broken and beaten miners. Media flooded the town and the world was introduced for the first time to the small town of Springhill, Nova Scotia.

Family, like Angus's sisters Francess Gillis, and Mary Soppa, his niece Vivian Canton, whom he named his baby girl after, fully pregnant and living in Amherst, gathered together at the old homestead, serving and working and praying. Giving up was not an option. No one knew that more than Nora Phalen Gillis, his wife. Never! One must never give up!

There is an indescribable feeling when a person finally sees the light, literally. Angus Gillis first saw the bright and overwhelming ray of light brought to him by a pick axe cutting through stone. His tears of relief were welcome and embraced by those whose hard work and resilience has paid off.

From 6000 feet below the surface to the top was a trip he would never forget.

Reunited with his family when so many of his peers weren't lucky enough to survive, Angus Gillis was truly grateful for all his blessings. It took a long time to recover from the after effects of the blast. Quite often he would take a walk down by the mines only to return filled with anxiety. The 39 friends and co-workers that died left an indelible mark on him. A changed man where the mines were concerned it took months and months to fully recover, if he ever really did.

The Number 4 Colliery never reopened. The men who lost their jobs were promised work in the Number 2. Some took the jobs and others didn't. Angus went back to work like any decent man would do for his family and he continued working until the Underground Bump of 1958 when it was decided that the mines would permanently close. He might have been one of the ones killed in that Bump had he not worked the opposite shift that day. Angus Gillis had seen a lot in his life. He grew up during the First World War, suffered though the Depression, fought in the second World War leaving behind a wife and small son. He said goodbye to his parents, lost brothers to the ravages of the coal mining life and yet there still seemed so much to be grateful for.

Of all the things that young Vivian knew there was something she realized during this tragic time that perhaps she never fully understood, and that is the true meaning of resilience and tenacity. It did not take her long to see that she was a part of a very big picture. Her family, especially the women played just as big a role in the coal mining industry as the men did. They all stood to lose as much as the men did. As she stood along side these fascinating women she soon realized that she was one of them as well. Vivian watched the town, her town come together in a time of tragedy and despair, how proud it made her feel inside.

Coal Mining in Nova Scotia, a hard old life. It took it's toll on so many families, those above and below ground. In 1964 Angus Gillis, like so many other valiant and courageous men of the deep mines said goodbye to his loving Nora, son Sam and a young Vivian Gillis whose was his very heart and soul.

Todd Canton & Vivian Gogan
Angus Gillis (1906-1964)

As The Snowflakes Gently Fall

On January 25th, our mother, Vivian Gillis would have been eighty years old. I don't know that many eighty year olds but the few I do, given their perspectives on life, seem to give new meaning to the term old age. My mother would have been one of those.

Her youthful and vibrant outlook on life is what I miss the most. She passed away at 71 from ALS. She wasn't the only one who battled the dreaded disease, we all did and we all lost.

She, Vivian Gillis, was the glue that held our family together. She, a force to be reckoned with, would have embraced her eighties like she did every event in her life, with enthusiasm and interest. Where will all this take me? I can hear her saying those words. We, her children, don't view life in the same way. I think basically in a youthful world we don't want to be reminded that we are getting older. We deny any aches and pains and do our best to get through the day. Our mother would march forward. She only looked forward. I never remember her saying 'when I was a girl this happened or that happened"... except maybe that chastity played a major role and one didn't dare act inappropriately.

Her optimistic attitude was something she says she inherited. Raised by coal miners in a mining town brought a realistic and down to earth approach to life. Those brave men, her heroes, faced death and destruction daily and they never gave up so why would she. Facing widowhood she felt the same way. It was not her choice to be left alone to raise a large family and yet she never walked out the door like a lesser woman might. She was fat from having kids and so something had to be done about it. There wasn't a gym, or a fat burning product available but there was sheer determination. She had lots of that. Looking back she set a real example of what a survivor was, a maverick.

If she was here she would tell you that the women in her family set a great example of courage and resilience. Mary Soppa, Nora Gillis, Sadie Henry, and Francess "Nan" Gillis. She learned from them. The one she should have been able to depend on, her own mother, abandoned her at birth, leaving

her to find her own wayin the world. She did. In fact, she created a world in which we were all born into, and she embraced each and every one of us in such a special way that we all suffer in silence at her leaving us. While we all have each other to lean on it still leaves a tinge of sorrow in our souls.

As the snowflakes gently fall and time marches on, Iam reminded that snowflakes aremeant to stand among and enjoy, that thunderstorms are a reason to open the front door and watch the brightly lit sky illuminate, to enjoy the sound of the pounding rains, the whistle of the winds and the warmth of a sunny day with which I can hear our mother say "Go outside and chase yourselves around."which really meant enjoy life and all it has to offer. Make the best of it.

Love you much, miss you more.
All of us!

As the Crow Flies

My backyard is a veritable playground for birds and small wildlife. One never knows what they will see when you look out my kitchen window. Wild partridges are abundant at this time of year. The neighborhood cat usually frightens them off. Then there's the sparrows, the starlings, beautiful blue jays, wild canaries, you name it. Most of them take advantage of our trickling pond and all it has to offer. It must be fascinating as our cat never leaves the window, she enjoys the show.

Once in a while a deer or two will wander through our property looking for fallen apples. But it is a squirrel that has made it's home in the neighbor's barn that fascinates me the most. What a busy little guy he is scampering about our yard, gathering scraps of food that he can store to get him through the long winter. That's one thing man and animal have in common, we are all trying to weather the weather.

Last Sunday during a routine clean up in the kitchen there was a bag of unused home-made bit & bites that would not likely be of any use to anyone. So, I thought the birds might like it and they tend to make the best of anything at this time of year. It cannot be easy for them..

So, I use my best arm to hurl handfuls of this rather tasty snack as far up the hill as I can. If it's too close to the house it may go unnoticed so I did my best to get it into the clearing. Not a bird in sight. Well, I thought to my self, it'll take a little time but someone will discover it. Well, not too long afterward, the little squirrel came gliding down the hills of white and JACKPOT! Pine nuts and peanuts and hickory sticks and pretzels and cheezies, what more could a hungry soul ask for? The first thing he did was taste a cheezie, it must've tasted good because he grabbed the next one in his cheeks and up the hill he went straight to his home in the barn. Back and forth the little prince scampered filling his cheeks and returning to his nest. Before long a bird or two noticed the orange dots in the snow and swooped down for a treat. First a mourning dove who cooed at the very sight of the feast and then let it known to her friends what was upon them. Then a blue jay, these birds are famous for chasing all others away but this guy wasn't true to form. He kept a respectful distance from the others. All is well. Then, as fate would have it, the neighbor's cat spotted the clutch of fowl and did his best to make his way down the snowy hill through the crunchy stuff, of course, giving himself away. Off they flew, no massacre here thank goodness. I guess cats don't care for bits & bites so he didn't stick around for long. The feast resumed.

But as the crow flies it is usually a warning to all. Danger is near. These birds are big as chickens, the menace of the sky, terrorize the neighborhood, tear open garbage bags, threaten the existence of all those who live around them. No wonder Alfred Hitchcock chose the likes of them to terrorize movie audiences. I think they would love to have feasted on a little squirrel gumbo and probably would have had they not noticed the strewn about treats. So as fate would have it, the rest of this food was cleaned up by these massive scavengers leaving nothing but a hint of orange dust on the crusty snow. But I will tell you one thing, there's one fat and happy little squirrel in a cozy barn up the hill.

More Coal

When a young Vivian Gillis left the town of Springhill, Nova Scotia in 1948 to be married, she so looked forward to her new life, and yet longed for home. The close knit ties of a coal mining family are carefully interwoven and uneasy to sever, perhaps due to a lot of pain and anguish. The kind of pain and anguish that goes along with the tragedies afforded coal mining families.

Raised by a spinster aunt in her grandmother's house, Vivian Gillis was made to feel like she belonged, and yet knew there was a different or better life for her. After graduation, she moved to Amherst to work. Aunt Francess told her to watch herself. " There's no need of you coming home in a year with a baby" and there wasn't. As a clerk in a hardware store, Vivian Gillis excelled. Her quick wit and outgoing personality was popular with the public, and before long she was making a name for herself as a knowledgeable and intelligent young woman. Something Francess Gillis knew from the very beginning.

A hateful and bitter woman in her fifties, Francess Ann Gillis, was truly unhappy with the choices she had made in her own life and did not want the same for Vivian. Nan, as Francess became known to all, made the mistake of having a baby out of wedlock in the 1930's when such a thing was unheard of. She had a daughter of her own, who in her own right was beautiful and intelligent, but was still a reminder of mistakes made, and despising the after-effects of such a shameful thing withdrew into herself. Since then the world had to pay for Nan's mistake. Her sharp wit and acid tongue was a weapon she used frequently and fiercely. I guess it was easier to push people away and to hold them at bay rather than open your heart. She did, however, hold in high regard, her niece, Vivian. More like a daughter than her own, Francess grew to love and respect the young girl with coal black hair and hazel eyes. One whose beauty, inside and out, only added to the Gillis household. What Nan probably never realized was that she was in her own way a strikingly beautiful woman. Yet, for her life was passing by and she was forced into the role of care-giver, a matronly spinster, a role she never felt she deserved.

So when it came time for Vivian to leave home, it hit Nan the hardest. Would she ever say so, not likely. Nan would never stand in her way of her making a better life. She did make it clear that the 'door was always open', a tradition in coal mining families and a tradition in the Gillis family.

When Vivian Gillis met Bert Canton in the mid-forties it was obvious to one and all that wedding bells might very well ring. It had to be a church wedding because in the Gillis family, Catholicism was as present as brewed tea. St. John's Catholic Church in Springhill wasn't quite big enough to house all the Gillises and the Cantons, so Amherst's St. Charles Catholic Church would do. In November of 1948, the two of them stood proudly at the front of the church, filled with a real sense of family, and became man and wife.

Vivian's father Dan Gillis proudly walked his daughter down the aisle while his new wife Veronica and all of those who had a connection to the kind young woman, gazed with loving eyes to see their girl get married. Francess Gillis especially could not hold back the tears. Never one to emote, she did her best to keep herself composed. She knew that with Bert Canton, Vivian would have a good life, and yet she hated the thought of losing her forever. As Vivian Gillis approached her future husband at the alter, she paused in the aisle for just a moment and reached into her bouquet of bright red roses and pulled from it, a single carnation that she gently handed to Nan. Silence filled the church. All of those who knew the situation were quick to realize that without saying one word, Vivian Gillis, found a way to say thank you, thank you very much. An unexpected surprise to the spinster aunt who up until that time acted as though no one mattered to her.

As time moved on, the babies started to come. Life in Amherst offered more than that of Springhill so really there was no reason to look back. Life would only move forward. But, there is a special bond that cannot be broken when it comes to the close-knit ties of a coal mining family. Despite the fact that the Cantons welcomed her into the fold, Vivian longed for the company of the Gillises, especially Nan. There, in her kitchen, the round and plump spinster stared out the window thinking about days gone by and the after effects of those days. Her thoughts were filled with family, her parents, brothers and their wives, and the losses and gains they all experienced in the small town of Springhill.

Tragedy brought Vivian home. November, 1956, word came that the Number 4 Colliery had an explosion as bad as the one in 1891. Shivers ran up Vivian's spine. Fully pregnant with her fourth child, there was no question, home she would go. Nan was waiting for her, so was Nan's sister Mary and sister-in-law Nora. All of them were familiar with the dangers of the mines and had heard about the devastation that a mine explosion can bring. This was their first experience in such a crisis and all pulled together instinctively. Their father Dancin' Dan Gillis always told them how lucky they were to be born girls and to never marry a coal miner like their mother did. Yet, **COAL** is what made Springhill, it heated the homes, fed the families, kept them all going. Francess and Mary's brothers were all the men of the deep mines, it's the only life they knew.

To serve the community they opened up the family home on Lisgar Street, making sandwiches, brewing tea, offering a resting place for weary helpers. Dozens were killed and even more injured. Sleep was out of the question and although taxing on the average person, Vivian Gillis began to show signs of battle fatigue. Nan took her to the side telling her that she had done all she could do here and it was time for her to go home to her family. "You have to think about your own family now, we will take care of the rest" Vivian knew she was right. Home to Amherst, home to her children and soon, to a new face, that of a little girl.

As life moved forward and the people of Springhill dealt with the losses, it became more and more evident to Vivian that these really were her people and my, how proud she really was of each and every one of them. These very strong and resilient individuals were a true example of what makes heroes. Not just the draegermen who did the rescues but the bare faced miners who jumped in to help, the doctors, and the businessmen who abandoned their social roles to roll up their sleeves and pitch in. The women, whose job it was to worry and wait, and how they took care of business above ground. Not just in times of emergency, but everyday.

It was proven again a couple of years later when, with child once again, 1958 and the Underground Bump that killed so many men. Again they rose to the challenge and fought a battle that was bigger than all of them. Nobody would have blamed them if they gave up, yet that seemed out of the question. So as Vivian Gillis, and all the Gillis women, and the rest of the resilient women of Springhill stood side by side, giving, not taking, it became clearer than ever that this was where each belonged, with family.

Despite the fact that Nan is gone, she does not lie in a lonely grave. She is buried along side family with several generations of the Gillises. A proud and stubborn woman whose personality was as immense as her talent to breathe and to survive. Her natural beauty, long flowing black hair pulled up and pinned into a bun. A flowered body apron draped over a matronly dress. Despite the tough exterior, within her lie a heart of gold, carefully protected by sheer guts and little glory. Francess Ann Gillis, the original coal miner's daughter. I honestly love you, and I miss you.

Double Wedding

When a young Vivian Gillis moved from Springhill to Amherst to work, it was like any impressionable young woman going to a strange city, filled with adventure and hope for the future.

She was all grown up and her family couldn't have been prouder of her. She rose above being a miner's wife. She was an educated young woman who was fortunate enough to have the chance to venture out into the big world. Amherst and Springhill are only 16 miles apart but Amherst was a lot larger and there were certainly a lot more people there. She found a place to live and board and formed a lasting friendship with the family. The Goldsmiths were practicing Catholics like herself, and held family in high regard. The two daughters Marjorie and Patricia became like sisters to Vivian. This made life bearable as she so badly missed the family she left behind in the close knit coal mining community.

Vivian joined the workforce as a sales clerk in the hardware business. Douglass Hardware on Victoria Street in Amherst was a well respected and thriving business. She did her best to fit in. Vivian had quite an outgoing personality and it paved the way for her in a business world that was predominantly ruled by men.

Still she found her place. How to treat people was an asset but knowledge a better tool. She worked hard to learn as much about the hardware business as she could. Her efforts paid off one day in particular. As a customer approached the desk, she immediately asked him if she could serve him. He was quick to say he much preferred a male clerk. "Of course" she said and motioned for one of the boys to wait on the customer. Not one to show any kind of emotion to the public, she allowed the sexist remark to pass and buried her head in her work. After a question or two from the customer the young clerk approached Vivian for the answer. She complied. Again the young man had a dilemma and she then too was helpful. It was after a third request that the young man was quick to inform the customer and the entire listening audience, *"she knows more than me!"*

There's a lesson in there somewhere.

A young man who was working in the warehouse of Douglass Hardware took a liking to the bright young woman. He found her interesting. Her quick wit and outgoing personality was something that drew him closer to her. He, Bert Canton, was a shy individual who was mesmerized by this striking young woman. The two fell in love. By this time Patricia Goldsmith had met the man of her dreams, a Frenchman Rene Richard. Marjorie began dating Jack Lane and so there was no doubt about it, love was in the air. Talk of marriage between the three young women was a daily topic over coffee, who would be asked first?

Vivian Gillis and Bert Canton were well matched and in everyone's eyes, and it became evident that the two of them would eventually wed. Vivian herself knew this was the only man she would ever love. He wasn't like any of the others she had been associated with. There was definitely something in his expression that spoke directly to her. Despite their vast differences the two of them knew each other was the one.

Pat and Rene were anxious to get on with their lives. He so wanted to take her to his homeland in Quebec and she was willing to follow him wherever he went. So marriage plans were in the works. Despite the fact that the two came from totally different cultures, love conquered all. Rene gathered what family he had nearby and Pat did the same but it was when it was suggested that a double wedding take place that things really began to get moving. While not everyone might agree on more than one bride in the room, it turned out to be a great opportunity to get the two shyest men to the altar, while allowing two bright and intelligent women to do the same. Never was there an ounce of competition between the two, it really would be pointless.

As the November weddings drew near, Mrs Goldsmith sat Vivian down for a talk. "I just wanted you to know that since you don't have a mother of your own to see you proper, I will sit with pride and keep an eye on you like a mother would, because I would be proud to have you as a daughter." Such kind words on the woman's part only deepened the affection Vivian held for the whole family. Mrs Goldsmith opened her doors to the Gillis family and although Aunt Francess would never have admitted it, she too appreciated the gesture. She was after all, the one who raised Vivian when her mother saw it fit to exit the baby's life, leaving her in the hands of the Gillis family.

Their girl was getting married and this was a reason to rejoice. Everyone was so very proud of Vivian and the choices she made in life. She met a man they all approved of and that was not an easy feat in a family that never agreed. Still, there they all were, bursting with pride at such an event.

In the wee hours of a November morning, the Cantons, the Goldsmiths, the Richards, and the Gillis families all gathered at Saint Charles Catholic Church in downtown Amherst Nova Scotia, where Miss Patricia Goldsmith became Mrs. Rene Richard and Miss Vivian Gillis became Mrs. Bert Canton and the rest, Ladies and Gentlemen, is history, mine.!

I was told as a child that all of us kids were brought into the world by love and love alone and have been fortunate to have lived a life filled with a real sense of life, laughter and love.

A Mother's Soul

When a disease such as ALS strikes an undeserving person, it is difficult for all involved. ALS didn't just kill our mother, it took a very big chunk of our own lives. We, the seven natural children of **Vivian Canton** have suffered our grief in many ways over the years since her death. Let's face it, sooner or later everyone loses their mother. Our mother was 71 years old and to some, had lived a long life, but to us, well, we weren't quite done yet. We all thought she would be around for years to come.

Since I was the one that lived the farthest away, I was able to see significant changes in her when I did visit. I was uncomfortable seeing my big, strong mother in such a delicate way and I believe that she was just as uncomfortable being seen. We covered it all up with humor like we did everything in our lives, but still, facing a loved one's demise can be very trying.

I loved my mother for all the reasons a child loves their mother, because she was my teacher, my companion, my disciplinarian and my friend. Not unusual, right? I believe that it was a little deeper than that. I believe that it was because she was accepting of me and my thoughts, no matter how bizarre, that truly made me appreciate myself and continue to venture down the less traveled path. In fact, she encouraged it.

My mother never said, "you can't do that". She might say "don't do that or this might happen," or "do you really want to do that?" but these were more for safety reasons than dream crushing. She encouraged me in anything that I attempted and if I failed, discouraged any kind of self-pity and enforced the issue of "try it again". She spoke to each and everyone from a Mother's Soul. For all these things I am grateful. As I sit and write at this computer on a rainy Sunday, I didn't think I had anything to say. For some reason, when I am down the most, I turn to my mother and ask what she might say in this situation, and when this mood passes like every other one, I go back to being me, and doing what I do best.......reach out to people. I take the gift that God gave me and by telling my stories.

Thank you Mother, for more things than I could ever list on this page and for picking up and dusting off a clumsy boy who has love in his heart for a woman who never gave up on him.

frEaK

Growing up in the town I did and with the people I did, I can't say it was all roses and sunshine. It had it's moments but I didn't get to be who I am today without jumping at least a few hurdles. In the elementary school that I attended, I was able to successfully fill the shoes of my older siblings and to carry on the tradition of being, well, average. It was the year I attended grade six that was my defining moment as a human being.

There was a boy in the other grade six class who was a freak. He had an artificial arm. As far as I knew he couldn't talk normally or anything like that. He was what they all called him, a freak. In an effort to grow socially it was decided that the two grade six classes would combine for such subjects as music, art and gym. I hated all of these classes, mostly because I had no talent. I couldn't play any kind of instrument, couldn't draw anything worthwhile and I defiantly sucked at any kind of physical activities. The reason I say it that way was I never even gave it a chance so how could I know. I was, after all, my own worst enemy. Then we had to choose teams. Do you know where I am going with this? Yup! I was chosen last. What a great feeling that is. At least the freak was worse than me, but not by mush.

BJ made sure that I knew I was chosen last. There he was a good athlete, handsome and popular and always had money on him. We were lucky to have a nickel to spend on candy at Fred's store but BJ always seemed to have a 20$ bill. This he flaunted in front of us as well as the fact that I was chosen last. Although it was fast becoming, me and the fREaK, that were chosen last.

So there we are, sitting on the bench side by side, me and Arthur Edward Prendergast III, or ARTIE as his freakish family called him. Well too bad for you, I thought to myself, I am not going to play with you. One thing I did master over the years was sulking. I could do it for hours. All I had to do was concentrate on the one thing that didn't ever let me down, me. I simply would shut off the rest of the world and that was that. Nothing and I mean nothing, not a teacher or a friend could penetrate the stone wall that I had built around me. "If you play doubles with me against BJ in volleyball I will treat you at the dairy Queen." he suggested. "Huh?" I thought to myself. "What?' he repeated this offer and I simply could not refuse. After all, volleyball is not that hard and Dairy Queen, well there is nothing like it. Banana milkshakes and brazier burgers.

Over he goes to BJ and although I can't hear the conversation, I think I knew it's contents. Back he comes with BJ and one of his cronies. We begin. Well, I have certainly learned a lot in my life but not as much as I did that day. First off, a prosthetic arm can hit a volley ball with amazing power, a freak from the wrong side of the tracks has hidden talents and three, never to pass up a chance to go to the Dairy Queen. As we walked down the long hill and up the road toward town I got to know Arthur Edward Prendergast III, not as a disabled person, but as a human being. There was a heart beating in his chest, and a bright mind at work all the time. He was a human being after all. We talked about the hideous arm with the forceps at the end, and how he fell in front of the lawn mower when his grandfather was mowing the lawn. He also told me about how the doctor told his mother he would be better off in a special school within an asylum with others like *him* and how she refused to see him as anything but her little boy. You can imagine my surprise when he paid with BJ's crisp 20$ bill. It just goes to show folks, God doesn't make mistakes, people do.

Arthur is now a savvy business man who lives near Saint John and produces prosthetic limbs for children that are so real hardly anyone could tell the difference. I believe he is a millionaire, I can only wonder what BJ is doing today and me, well I'm just me.

Life is a Restaurant

A good server can make up for bad food but good food cannot make up for a bad server!
Jackie McKeown

I was hungry as a child. When one suffers any great deed as a little person it often leaves an unforgettable mark. I was hungry in both my tummy and my heart. I was hungry for attention and affection. I was hungry for acceptance. I found all of this in the hands and hearts of the public. To me life is a restaurant and our each and every move is in the menu. Breakfast, lunch and dinner. There's some things sweet and some tart. Some stuff there you will enjoy and some you will definitely stay away from. Correct?

I have to tell you, I love being a waiter. It has a lot to do with the fast pace, the hard work, the generosity of the people, and the food. I like food. I love good food. Probably because I was hungry as a child. We never had a lot. We never starved but I felt like there was always something missing. I still feel like something is missing from my menu. I have spent a lifetime looking for it.

Interacting with the public is something I am good at. I like to talk and I like to be listened to. I am honest in my approach to the table. I am not a smiler but people think I am. I do have a kind voice. To them it sounds like a smile. Whatever works. I make good suggestions and I do my very best to give them the most for their money. I learned a long time ago that if you take care of the customer, they will take care of you. I don't mean with just a tip but with a loyal following and a cultivated relationship based on respect. That is truly a great gift.

Customers of all ages come to our restaurant and I am able to speak to and interact with each and everyone of them on any level. It took me a while to get here but I did it. Most people think I am a natural but it is a craft and I have perfected it over the years. Inside I'm quite shy although anyone who knows me will not bear witness. I come from a shy and insecure family and I had a choice to stay in the dark or walk in the light. I chose the light. Inside I am of the thinking that when the time comes for me to die then I know that I will have lived a full life. I do not let much pass me by.

Take a moment to check out your menu. There's lots in there. Those who wish to lead a healthy lifestyle stroll through the whole grains and salads. Those who feel they want a little more sustenance head toward the burgers and fries. Fish and chicken are the likely choices today but there's lots of old fashioned meat and potatoes as well. My advice in this ever changing world is to try new things on the menu. Don't be fussy, do be particular. Appreciate the fact that your restaurant is in a free country and that your menu holds food from just about every culture and there is definitely something in there for everyone. Don't forget to drink milk and water and oh yeah, enjoy life.

At home we have one family and at work we have another family, of sorts. Some customers are held in high regard and they accept you as a friend and an extended member of their family. They look for you when they come in and comment on your not being here the last time they were in. It makes you feel good that you are appreciated.

Now, the reason for this story is to tell you about my friend, **Agnes "Beatrice Perry"Welsch**. She is a customer of mine and has been for as many years as I have been in the public. She is a mother and a grandmother and a widow. She is a loving daughter to her mother. When I first met her she walked leaning on a cane. Now she sits on wheels. To me she has a full life and lacks for very little. Somewhere along the line she developed an affection for me. She loves me like I was her own child and is not afraid to tell everyone in the room how she feels. She has done it on many occasions. Why she feels this way about me I am not so sure. I cannot recall an incident where I did anything special but somehow it happened. Her mother and her traveled together constantly. As her mother's years began to show, all could see her time was coming. Unexpectedly, Agnes took sick and her mother got stronger. This is what we refer to, in my family, as

You Needed Me. When her child was ill and required care, she summoned the strength from within. I have seen it happen on several occasions and I consider it to be nothing short of a miracle.

Both of these women are considered a part of my public family. I have never been to their homes nor have they been to mine but I truly believe each one of us would proudly welcome one another. I have never tired of listening to Agnes talk nor have I ever been anything but comfortable in her presence. I can't say that about very many people. She takes the time to tell me how much seeing me makes her feel happy and how my being who I am, makes her day. What she may not realize is how she makes me feel. I am so very undeserving of such praise. I am simply a good waiter who has done right by my customers. The fact that she holds me in such high regard truly escapes me but let me tell you something. On those days when I am just about ready to throw in the dishtowel, in she rolls full of hugs and compliments and takes my bruised and battered ego and sets it free. For that I am so very grateful.

I wanted to take the time to write this and to tell you about Agnes. She hasn't been feeling well lately and when she was in the restaurant on Saturday she said something to me that has haunted me ever since. I was busy. You know what I mean, busy. It was raining and that brought a lot of people in. I had so many milkshakes to make and so many people to serve. I was on alone and the cook was moody. I just about had enough and there was no one around to help me. Agnes told me her mother had passed away. I said I didn't know or I would have come. I don't even think I knew that woman's name. I always called her Mother. I wish someone would have told me. There wasn't much I could do but I would do what I could.

Agnes and her grown granddaughter ate and talked and as they were leaving, she slipped her hand into mine and said to me " I don't know when I'll see you again or if I ever will see you again so take care of yourself." I was quick to say what a survivor she was and that I knew she wasn't done yet. Something like that. What I didn't do was what I should have. I should have apologized to the room, got myself a hot cup of tea and sat down with her. I needed a break and she was the one there to remind me to take one, a break from life that is. Take a moment to sit and talk whether or not you think you have the time to do it. It might make the world of difference to you and the one you are talking to. Thank you Agnes "Bea

Perry"Welsch and Inez Perry for all that you do and all that you are. Thank you for making my restaurant a nice place to be. You make me want to be a better person.

And thank you to you Jackie for your continued support!

It Happened One Christmas

It was the first Christmas after our father's death that was the hardest to endure. He, a quiet and gentle man, enjoyed the festivities and his family get- togethers. We were all young when he passed away and the blow is pretty hard toward us, his children and toward his wife, a 43 year old mother of nine. Still our mother marched forward with a grand sense of who she was, and did what was necessary to feed and clothe her family.

I feel she was admired by our neighbors and friends for her sheer tenacity, but deep within her was a sense of pride that would not allow her to be a victim. So onward we went as a family with our mother at the helm. Christmas especially was a challenge but we got through it. We, the children were never fully aware of how financially strapped we were, mother didn't burden us with it. Myself and my sisters Anne and Ruth were really kept in the dark as we were the youngest. Mother thought this best.

As the fresh snow blew across the marsh toward our little piece of heaven, Christmas lights illuminated the skies and the sound of your favorite seasonal songs could be heard. Our house was warm and our mother even warmer. There she stood in the doorway waiting for each and every one of us making sure we were home and safe. And we were.

Just walking along the road toward home after school meant something as the winter settled in because it truly was beautiful. Snow was a large part of our lives and we accepted that. Our backyard was filled with drifts and became a veritable playground of snow forts and snowball fights. Those who were fortunate enough to own snowmobiles took advantage of the open pastures behind our home. The cool winds whistled among the trees and all of us were left with rosy faces and cold feet. To home we would go where *she* was, waiting.

Once our sister Edith arrived home from school in Sydney, it made it really feel like the holidays. We all had to be together or it just wouldn't be the same. He might not have been there but our mother kept us so busy running errands, like my sister Susan and I taking the long walk to Margolians to buy a tea cup and saucer for great-aunt Mary Soppa, to cleaning the house and helping to prepare the food for the most important meal of the year. Our oven roasted turkey with dressing and vegetables and cranberries and gravy. What a feast she would prepare and each of us helped in one way or another. The whole time she would remind us of how lucky we were and how not everyone would have a nice Christmas. Imagine that! She took our minds off our grief and off ourselves just long enough to appreciate what we had, not what we didn't have. As I ate our carefully prepared dinner I thought to myself "Does every Christmas table have dishes that don't match?" well, it didn't matter because dishes don't make a meal, the food does.

The weather man always predicts snow for our area but that year there seemed to be more of it. We were blanketed with plenty of the white stuff and it invited us outside. Friends came over and all of us made the best of the winter at hand. On Christmas Eve just as the sun had gone down, my sister Susan heard a rustling in the back porch. Not opening the door herself she let our mother know that we had company. Not on a night like this, surely, we all thought. Who could it be? It was Christmas Eve and nobody drops by, they all should be home with their families. In the darkness of our back porch we could all see the huge package that someone dropped off. It was a collection of boxes of cereal, homemade knitted mittens, bags of penny candy, chips, a Christmas ornament and a few other essentials.

Mother opened the porch door only to see the silhouette of a man with his hood up to guard against the wind and to shield his face from us. He cut across the pasture toward Copp Avenue and in a moment he was gone from view. Not one of us spoke as our brother Jack carried the parcel inside and set it at our mother's feet.

Such kindness on that man's part. He probably never knew how remarkable a gift he gave us as a family, opening our eyes to the true meaning of Christmas. I am sure in the silence of his own home, sitting down with his family that Christmas Eve, and all the other Christmas Eves that followed, looking into the faces of his children and into the eyes of his wife, he must've held appreciation for all he had. How very fortunate for us, a fatherless family, that we were on his mind and in his heart. I don't think his family ever knew the story until now because that's the kind of man he was.

That man was Les Ayer. (July 27, 1924 to May 3, 2007)

Jack Rabbit

This story is part of a series of stories for young hearts and was inspired by a boy I knew with big ears....

When they're born they call them bunnies and when they're grown they call them rabbits, that's just the way it is. Growing up on the Tantarmar marshes was very interesting to this particular clutch of bunnies. Lots to do, lots to see and lots of others to play with. Generations of our family lived on the marsh, our grandparents, our parents and us. It is great to have family around because it is from them that you learn how to survive in this world. Our mother took care of all of us and there were lots of us too and it seemed we all looked alike and I guess that's okay. All in all it was a happy life, no one ever thought of leaving the marsh but things change when you grow up.

One day a bunny from away dropped by to play and he was interesting to us because he seemed to know so much more than we did. He traveled a lot and saw lots more of our vast marsh than we ever did. I guess in a way it made him more worldly and sophisticated. As we were all busy running around playing and jumping he took a long look at us and said "Who's that?" pointing to my brother Jack. "He sure does have big ears" Now this came as a bit of a shock as we never really noticed the fact that Jack had big ears until this stranger pointed it out, but Jack did indeed have bigger ears than all of us. Realizing this was not funny rather sad to know that this made Jack different from the rest of us. We didn't want him to feel different, or to have his feelings hurt, he was after all, our brother.

In my heart I was sad because this stranger was making fun of one of us so I went to talk to Mother about it. She explained the whole situation to me knowing very well how upset I got over things like that. Jack looks the way he does for a reason, he inherited his look. "Who is the greatest man you know?" she asked and I was quick to reply "Grampie" and he was. "Well take a look at his ears sometime, he has big ears too so you don't have to worry about Jack, he will be fine, after all he is carrying on a family tradition." And he is.

Winters can be wicked on the marsh that's why we all have to cuddle. Our mother keeps us very close and that is a nice feeling. Heavy snowfall blows in over the marsh covering everything in it's path. It's great to play in. Summers are warm and nice. This summer was a particularly dry one. This worries Mother although she never talks about it. She just stares out into the horizon watching first at sunrise and then at sunset. I could feel the twigs snap beneath my feet as I walked along the trail. We knew never to venture very far from our mother or she would come and get us and bring us back. All she ever wanted was for us to be safe. When I went down to the river for a drink I was surprised to find it had gone dry. This never happens but as I said this summer was a dry one.

As the warm breeze blew gently across the marsh there was in the distance the usual clatter from our friends and neighbors, other bunnies our age running and jumping and playing. From behind me off in the distance I could see Jack running toward us. He had look of sheer terror on his face. He flew past me and the others and ran right to our mother. With one word from his mouth our lives would change forever. Fire!

My mother stomped her foot three times. This was not a test it was the real thing. In an instant we as a family came together and flew as quickly as we could off the marsh and up the field and ran and ran until our mother was sure that we were safe. My heart was beating so loudly in my ears that I could not see or hear clearly. I was frightened for my life and for good reason. The fire spread quickly over the entire marsh and destroyed everything in it's path. Homes were gone, food, and unfortunately some lives too. But our mother had brought all of her bunnies to safety and as we looked at all the devastation on the marsh and up at the smoke-filled sky we knew that we were alive because our brother Jack, the one with the big ears, heard the crackling of the fire before anyone else did and ran to warn our mother. Jack Rabbit saved the day.

Since we lost everything each one of us was to make a new start. It was decided by our mother that a lot of work had to be done and if this meant separating then that's what we had to do. Jack was the oldest boy so he went first. He was told that there were bigger greener fields over the hill and so he set out to find them.

Our mother never wanted to let us go but she wouldn't stand in our way either. We got word that Jack had indeed found greener pastures and decided to make a home for himself there. We all wished him well.

The rest of us bunnies spread out all over the place looking for work and we all found it in one form or another.

Our mother taught us early on that hard work and perseverance would get you anywhere. She was right.

It was when our mother took sick that each and everyone of us stopped and took the time to go and see her. Jack Rabbit sat quietly beside our mother whose time was near. He talked to her in a soothing way reminiscing about our days on the marsh and what it was like growing up the way we did. Mother liked it when Jack would visit. She loved all her children in different ways and that is a nice thing.

When our mother died one spring day each of us grieved in our own way. It didn't do any good to hold in the pain because she was, after all, our mother. We all stood there the last day and said goodbye to her in our own way. We all suffered from the same ailment, broken hearts. You and me and our brother **Jack Rabbit.**

Life With Brian

The year my father died was one of the worst of my young life, of course. When Bert Canton passed away in May, I was eleven years old, grade six. The whole summer that year was an emotional one for me, to say the least. When I went to grade seven in September, I was still eleven years old. Big school, even bigger kids. That was not a welcoming adventure for me to take. Still, out the door I went everyday at my mother's urging, me hoping someday the sun would shine again and she, hoping I would find happiness in the big world. Unexpectedly, I was able to find a bright spot or two during that time.

Grade seven was tough because I wasn't the best student and then there is the loss one suffers when you leave the security of elementary school where you know all the kids, to tackling junior high where you really come face to face with strangers. Some lasting friendships form and others fall by the wayside.

My association with Brian Ripley was such a friendship. While I was afforded a life in town, he was a country boy. I walked to school and back, while he took a bus. While not everyone was fond of country folk, all of us seemed to find our place in the class system at Amherst Regional High School. Mrs Pipes was our teacher, a genuinely nice lady. She treated each and every student fairly. This is something we all noticed from the very beginning that no matter who you were, it seems you were welcome in her classroom.

Brian stayed for lunch at school while I was able to walk home. So every once in a while I invited him home with me. Down Spring Street to Church, across Albion to Crescent Ave., and then to Station Street, down

Victoria to the store and then follow the path to Russell. A long walk, a long talk. We, the Cantons, never had a lot but we always had enough, and there was certainly always room for one more at our table. The table my father fashioned years before and a bench along the wall below the window so that all of us kids could cram together and feast. Brian brought with him his manners and a clean face, we shared with him our food, our hospitality and our sense of humour. He seemed to enjoy that. He did, after all, come back again.

Then it was my turn. He insisted I go to his family's home overnight. Overnight? Oh, no, not likely. Our mother never let us an arm's length away from her and I am sure she wouldn't allow this. "Go" she said "and have a good time." I took her to the side, "What if I wet the bed? I would die of embarrassment!" "You won't!" she said "you are too scared to wet the bed in someone else's house, and besides, you haven't done that in a while". "Like it or don't you are growing up." I guess at that very moment I was, growing up, I mean.

Out to the country I went with Brian on his bus. To a real farm no less. They had cows and chickens and barns and hay and massive woods around them. It was a real dream come true for me. It was also an eye opener. This was a true country family that went to church on Sundays, said grace at the table and held a real sense of family values. The mother Bonnie was the nicest woman in the world, the father Rupert, a quiet and reserved man. Brian had two brothers and a sister, Kevin and Donna Lee and a little brother Eric. I liked them right away. Brian found them annoying as he was the oldest. As a result of his being the first, he held a certain responsibility to uphold the Ripley name and keep it in good standing. He did so. Any father would be proud to have a son like him. Father, oh yes, I no longer had one.

Brian may have been annoyed by his siblings but I found them interesting, as I was a middle child and they reminded me of my own family. Also, there was a big difference, there weren't as many of them. So that meant, when we sat down to eat there was plenty and I mean plenty. At meal time in our house, we were warned not to take too much if there was company because we absolutely did not want to run out. It wasn't that way out there.

The whole time I visited I, had a gnawing feeling in my stomach. As nice as this family was I still wanted to go home. It was Friday night and that was the night we *"sent out"*. That means our mother would splurge and we would get some hamburgers from Tubby's or a snack from Dixie Lee. It was a very special time for me and I was missing it. And then, what if I couldn't sleep? I was filled with a secret sense of dread for the night ahead.

Oh well, just make the best of it and when it's over, you never have to do it again. That's what I kept telling myself.

As evening set in Bonnie told us she had some errands in town and did we want to come? I went along with them. What I didn't know was that it would take me near to home in a way. We went to Brain's grandmother's house. Bonnie's mother, another Mrs Ripley. She lived on Victoria Street not far from Russell. I could see my house from their yard. We got there around nine PM and Mrs Ripley was waiting. She welcomed me into the fold as if I was one of her own grandchildren. Not only was her home warm and inviting but she put before us, a feast. On a long dining room table there was turkey, mashed potatoes, roast beef and ham, carrots and peas. To the side was jams and jellies and biscuits. Milk to drink. This was a meal fit for a king. It reminded me of years before going to Springhill with Mom and Dad and the feasts that the Gillis's and the Soppas would prepare. In it's own way it all took me home. I sat and ate until I was cross-eyed and then we went for the long drive home, tired.

I slept like a baby. Upon awakening in the morning no one was more surprised than me that there was no wet spot. So far, so good. So, there we were in the fresh Nappan air, out to the barns, to do chores. I didn't know what I was doing but I did the best I could do, and then breakfast. . Later that afternoon Brian's mother dropped me off at home I regaled my mother with all I had experienced. That was the beginning of many visits back and forth. Brian Ripley was my best friend. He accepted me for the misfit I was and I accepted him for who he was. Isn't that what true friendship is all about?

Brian's and my friendship grew over the next year and a half but when we went to grade eight he wasn't in the majority of my classes. We may not have interacted on a daily basis in school but we certainly did on the weekends. His parents took us to the shore and that was great. We spend many hours trekking through the woods near his home and at mine, enjoying the breathtaking beauty of the Tantramar Marsh.

As fate would have it, Brian and I grew apart. It wasn't that we had different interests, it wasn't that we didn't like the same music, or even the distance between our homes, we met girls. Quite often friendships fall by the wayside when a woman enters the picture. He met the Newcombes and I met the Benjamins.

As a family, we had no money so my teenage years were spent working. If you wanted anything of value one had to work and so I did. That's when I met my future wife. By this time Brian had met and married the love of his life and they had a baby, a boy. Work was available in the Valley and they moved there. One Christmas, some ten years after we had met. Brian and his wife were killed in a snowstorm on their way home after Christmas. The boy, Nathan, was the only survivor of the crash. He has subsequently been raised by Brian's parents.

Despite the roads I have traveled and the people I've met, and there have been plenty. I will never forget Brian Ripley, his family, their kindness, generosity or his smile. Brian you were a bright spot in a very dark period of my life. Thank you.

Giant of a Woman

Fate can be cruel. It's not fair for an eleven year old boy to lose his father to Cancer. I also don't think it's fair for a 43 year old woman to be a widow with a houseful of kids to raise alone. Hey, we've all got our sad stories, this is mine.

If I can take my selfish ego outside of me for a moment, I will share with you the events surrounding the death of my father. I was eleven years old in grade six, it was May. As the school year was wrapping up, all of us in Mr Hunter's class were nervously anticipating going to grade seven at the high school. My father had been sick but I was unaware how really bad it all was. His death came as a great shock to me. How the rest of my family was dealing with it was oblivious to me at the time as I was numb..

Our mother, now there's a piece of work. She was the "love child" of Kathleen McKenna and Dan Gillis. That's a nice way of saying she was illegitimate. My grandparents never married. He married someone else and she left town, never to be heard from again. As a result my mother was raised in her grandparent's home in Springhill, with a spinster aunt at the helm. Despite humble beginnings, the little girl flourished. She met and married my shy father and began a life filled with children. We became all she lived for.

Since she invested so much time in all of us, she neglected herself. Gray before her time, our mother also gained a significant amount of weight. He lost interest in her and although it spelled disaster for her marriage, she continued with her life filled with the happy and unhappy sounds of children.

When he passed away she saw it fit to protect her youngest children, of which I was one, from any further emotional abuse by sheltering us. Not permitted to attend our father's funeral, she thought it best to reside with family friends for the day. We did as she asked. What she didn't realize was this was going to affect us later. She sent us to the outskirts of town which happened to be across the corn field from the graveyard where my father lays buried. From the back yard standing on a pile of lumber I was able to view the funeral procession that I really should have been a part of. There in the crowd was my grandfather with his head bowed and my father's brothers and sisters, a sad lot. But in my mind is etched forever, my mother, a giant of a woman. There she stood, tall and strong, going through the motions, taking care of business. In a moment, standing there on a hot May afternoon, something inside me changed. I was no longer a sniveling little boy, my eyes began to open. My eyes and heart were opening to the world around me and it all began to unfold.

I was able to see past the exterior of this magnificent creature and to see for myself what a strong and independent maverick she really was. My mother was a force to be reckoned with, a brave soldier who fought to survive and a resilient and tenacious character that I grew to immensely respect. That ladies and gentlemen is something that I carry in my heart today.

My Funny Valentine

A little over thirty years ago in Cecil's Restaurant and Home Bakery on Victoria Street in downtown Amherst, Nova Scotia, I met the girl I would fall in love with, the woman I would marry and the best friend I will ever have. Now those of you who cannot take a little romance, I suggest you turn the page.

Sherry Lee Benjamin was the quietest, nicest girl I have ever met in my life. Since growing up in a house full of independent women led by an domineering mother, I must say I found her quite refreshing. After taking the time to get to know her, I found the true sense of who I really am.

Sherry Benjamin was a girl who was definitely out of my league. She was smart, intelligent, athletic and beautiful. I was sixteen, six feet tall with a caved in chest, long hair and pimples. Who wouldn't want me? Sherry's grades were excellent, and her organizational skills unmatched, mine were not. She was a great cook, a neat and tidy person and she was quietly taking over my heart. Her sense of humor only added to the demure loveliness that sat before me. Such blue eyes, such a precious demeanor, I tell you people, I fell in love.

It got so bad over the next couple of years that the two of us only had eyes for each other. This was much to the dismay of our friends and families. My mother once commented that we were **"like a couple that had been married for fifty years, quite often finishing each other's sentences, saying the same things at the same time and laughing hysterically at the same things"**. She became a part of me and I a part of her. Sounds corny to say, doesn't it?

After a couple of years of this relationship, I, feeling a little restless, thought the grass was greener on the other side and as a result she gave me freedom,. It wasn't long before I found that there was no one out there like her and it didn't take much before I crawled back to her, with ring in hand. I knew without a doubt that she was the only one for me. Even at our young age, it was so veryclear that love was what she quietly brought into every room she entered, in everything she did for me, and that by keeping me constant in her thoughts was cementing our lives together, forever.

Coming from the close knit family that I did, I suspected that I would marry a woman who filled my house with children, this didn't happen. Her family life at home was difficult so she knew it was inevitable that she move on and in doing so, took me by the hand. I followed her into a very private and personal existence that she shares with few.

Recently, we celebrated our twenty- fifth anniversary and I must tell you. I don't know where the years went. I have never tired of looking into those blue eyes, asking her opinion, or reaching out for her. I could never see me sitting on the porch swing with anyone but her.

She has taken the house we bought and made it into a home. The two of us have no children so our pets get the love and affection that children would receive. She is a talented chef, a master builder, a diligent worker who finishes what she starts, and she inspires me to write nice things, to look for the beauty in nature, to appreciate the animal kingdom, and to cherish life. That ladies and gentlemen, is a lovely and wonderful thing.

My Grandmother's Kitchen

When my grandmother was in her late seventies she began to show signs of decline. While this is not unusual, it wasn't easy for us as a family to witness. I was eight years old when I really took notice of what a wonderful woman she really was. Funny and entertaining, she always had an interesting story to tell.

Her place was in the kitchen. There in her cupboards were neatly arranged rows of tea cups and saucers. In a drawer were perfectly folded tea towels and dish clothes, some of them twenty or so years old. A place for everything and everything in it's place. In the brightly lit corner of the kitchen near a window, was her sewing area. On the tiny table were her glasses and next to them, her bible. Some days were filled with sewing and others reading the written word. She found comfort in both.

On her stove was a continuous full pot of steeped tea. "That reminds me," she said out loud. "Granville's has tea on sale today, I must get Papa some". Then, a little embarrassed, she realized that Papa was not with us anymore. She looked down into my face and said. "I'm so used to having him around, that I forget that he's gone." I knew she wanted to cry but what good would that do? Back to her cooking.

Our grandmother was good at everything she did. Her house was always neat and tidy, her back yard neatly manicured and her life itself was orderly and old fashioned. It was however, her cooking skills that were the envy of the neighborhood. There was no longer any reason to open her cookbooks as she had mastered all of the recipes. Anything from a simple meatloaf to a full Roasted turkey dinner with all of the trimmings, each and every meal was a masterpiece.

Through the window you could see how healthy her garden was. This year we had the perfect amount of rain so everything was coming along nicely. As she looked out she thought to herself. I wonder if this is the last year I will spend in this house. Since Papa had died the year before, she was lonely, not sad. She busied herself with cooking for the neighbors or for fund raiser for the church. Homemade pickles and preserves, jams and jellies and of course, her famous fruitcakes.

When our sister married an Acadian, she whipped up a pot of pea soup. While a few in the family turned their nose up at such a delicacy, most thoroughly enjoyed it. He especially enjoyed the friendly gesture an asked her if she would like to adopt him as her grandchild. "I already did" was her reply.

On the day she died it was like any other June day, a soft breeze blowing across a cluster of mayflowers that had bloomed in the morning sun.. Wheat toast for breakfast, a hot cup of tea to go along with it, biscuits in the oven. As she stood to check on her cooking, the angels swept in and in a moment she softly floated to the floor. Never one for much fanfare nor a burden to anyone, she left the world the same way she entered it, quietly, taking our hearts with her.

Mothers Control the Pages Of Time

When Springhill born singer Anne Murray burst onto the music scene, no one, not even Anne herself would ever have believed the success she would achieve, or that she would still be held in such high regard today. Well, maybe her mother did. It seems **Marion Murray** saw something special about her daughter way before anyone else ever did. This, I believe, has allowed Anne to reach amazing heights. Wouldn't we all if our mothers showed us such support?

Let's face it. Not everyone had a good childhood. Not everyone's parents stayed together and not all of us were family oriented. Some of us could hardly wait to get out from under our mother's thumb. Not me of course! I liked living with a domineering mother and many, many sisters so that I could successfully find my sensitive side. And let me tell you this folks, if I get any more sensitive......hmmmm....

Working in the school system I am privy to all sorts, of mothers I mean. Big ones, small ones, fat ones, tall ones. They all have one thing in common. Power. When mother comes through the door, look out. Most mothers are very busy people and when duty calls at school, this means business.. You get your kind, your cranky, you get your long and lanky, you get your single, and your married, your calm and your harried. All have one thing in common. Justice. Maybe the problem is the school's fault, the kids fault, or even the mother's fault but, once it's addressed, it's supposed to go away. hmmmm.....

The stage mother from long ago stood in the wings and pushed the kid onto the stage with great hopes of them achieving fame and fortune.

Frowned upon by the public, this type of mother soon faded, or did she? hmmm........

Then there's the sports MOM, she can holler louder than most folks. She wants her kid, however inept, to win. She'll tell you she just wants him to have fun and to do his best, but I think she sees a trophy on the mantle. My sister Susan was such a mother. Her son Jeffrey was an excellent baseball player. She would sit in the stands and holler. Once she hollered at the coach for getting after her son. This totally embarrassed Jeffrey and so the war was on between the two when they got home. To him the coach was GOD, she was only Mom. hmmm...

Mother knows best. Kinda like my own mother who for years hollered up the steps for Jack, my brother, to get up for school. It seems he wasn't a morning person! At one point he growled at her wanting to know why she wouldn't get off his back. She in turn reminded him of how important an education was, and that it was a must that he receive one. The fact that he criticized her efforts spent on his behalf, sent her into a frenzy of rage where she told him that "when the diploma is passed out at the end of the year, it had better have my name on it!"hmmm....

Mothers have been known to perform great feats for the sake of their children. We've all heard the stories of women who have lifted vehicles off of their children or who have run into burning buildings to save their offspring and come out unscathed. It is a power that is too big to explain. The same power can be scathing if you turn your mother against you. Look out, then you've really started something. In grade six my mother received a phone call from my teacher who said I talked too much, hurried through my work so I could talk some more, and as a result of my talking, constantly interrupted the class. It seems she had a similar problem with my brother some ten years earlier. Her solution to that was for the teacher to take the yard stick and hit the desk of the boy next to him and tell them all to keep quiet and get to work. Singling out my very shy brother might devastate the poor thing. My mother's solution for me, strap him! hmmm.....

So there you go folks, as the pages of time turn before us, I am continually amazed that as different as the generations are, there still remains a constant in our lives. Mother. So as the song "Mama" goes "Some have a good one and some have a bad one, but all of God's children have got to have had one Mama at one time." and were all still here, she never killed us yet, imagine that!

Take care and be well

The Thought of Anne

Our sister Anne was our mother and father's *love* child. It brought them closer together than they had ever been after a few emotional setbacks. It may have had something to do with the fact that Mother nearly died giving birth to Anne, or the fact that Dad had finally found true love in the face of our mother. Either or, it happened. Both were quick to be reminded just how precious life is.

We, as a family, are not jealous of the fact that Anne was our mother's favorite. We all can see her special qualities. If any of us was having a knock down, drag 'em out fight, it was never with Anne. She was, if I dare say, the fawn of our family. A kind and gentle soul who devoted her life to one thing, loving our mother.

Mother never gave her things that she didn't give us, she never filled her bowl more than she did ours, it was more the fact that Anne seemed to appreciate our mother more than we did. When it came to Mother's Day or her birthday, Anne would find the tenderest card. The words on the page would tell our mother how much she loved her and those words were true. Anne's heart was always filled with thoughts of our mother. At least it sure looked that way.

Anne embarrasses easily. She is such a gentle and shy soul, one really doesn't want to offend her. If you did, your conscience would get the best of you. You really don't want to hurt Anne's feelings, that just wouldn't be right. Mother would be mad at you and the rest of us might pound you when we get you alone. " Leave her alone", we would say, "she never hurts anybody". And she didn't.

After school we would all run home so we could play. Our life was spent outside. Sledding, tobogganing, skating. Anne might very well sit inside and read her homework to Mother and talk to her about what kind of day she had. Mother always seemed to enjoy that.

Anne would stay by our mother's side when she was preparing supper. Always helpful, she did the best job that a daughter could do. This only deepened Mother's affection for Anne. Mother would often tell us about the day the doctor said that she might have to make a choice over her own life or that of her child. Our mother was quick to say "Save my child, my husband is a good man, he'll marry again." Our father, on the other hand, said, "Save my wife, I cannot raise six kids on my own." You know something? He would have resented Anne had she caused our mother's death. It's a good thing it worked out the way it did. I guess when he held her in his arms for the first time he told our mother. "This one is fragile," and she was. Fragile and strong at the same time. Like our mother, Anne survived against the odds.

This was proven all too recently when our mother was diagnosed with, and consequently died from ALS. Anne took care of her. She washed and brushed her hair, and changed her clothes. She sat up at night and talked to and read to our mother. Both Anne and our sister Ruth did such a grand job taking care of her that I find it very difficult to criticize either of them whenever they mess up, and let me tell you something folks, that's not very often.

We all kind of agree that Anne should have been a nurse. She has such a caring way about her. She never had any babies of her own but she had babies in other ways. They love her as much as she loves them. Love is what is in her heart. Our Anne's been a little lonely of late, Mother is gone, Stacie's kids are out west and she finds herself working all the time. Anne likes to keep busy, it takes her mind off things.

As far as this all goes, I just wanted to say: Anne, you've been on my mind lately, and I wanted to find a way to say..................thanks for making each and everyone of stop and smell the roses. It seems that you have become the rose in all of our lives.

just your brother,
Todd

The Songs in my Heart

This is probably the most personal thing that I, Todd Canton, have ever written.

I was eleven years old when my father died. Grade six. West Highlands School, Amherst, Nova Scotia, Canada. His death made such an impact that I am quite sure that thirty years later that I am not entirely over it. I remember school at the time because I felt that it was the most important thing in my life. My father's death interrupted my educational process, my personal life and me, the little boy who was left without a father, I was lost.

When you lose someone who sits down at your table there is an emptiness that finds it's way inside of you. That emptiness for me was a strong feeling of despair So much so that I wished that I could die so that I would not have to endure those feelings any longer. I didn't want to die in the same sense my father did. I just did not want to feel anything anymore. I wanted the world to go away. As a Catholic it was my first instinct to pray. I prayed to God to let me hear or see a sign of hope. Since I was unable to sleep at night, I found myself quite often gazing up at the beautiful summer skies. The view from my bedroom window was able to fully capture the vastness of the Tantramar marshes. It was then that I knew the truth. In my dreams my father was so near. In my sleep he was where he should be on my mind, in my heart but physically....he was gone. In the quiet beauty of the silent evenings I wished upon star after star that some other kind of life form, an alien life-form or an angel, would land quietly and rescue me from the pain and suffering I endured at such a young age.

I also lived through fantasy, you know the kind, where my father was on a secret mission for the Canadian government and he had to be dead in order for all of us to be safe. Then one day a helicopter would land in the tall grass near our home and our father would quietly slip into our home and back into our lives, even if it meant he was going to leave on another mission. At least I would see him again. This of course, never came to be.

It was my mother who was able to soothe my aching soul. A widow at forty-three, a mother of seven, and a my saving grace, she was the one who knew me best, although I wonder now if she even realized the positive impact that she made on me. I remember me as a complicated little boy.

My mother bought me a radio for my room and with it came headphones. She was always one to encourage us to get to know the world around us. Many of my sleepless nights were spent listening to All Night Radio from New York or, if the night was clear, just about anywhere in the world. With that small contribution from my mother she opened up a whole new world to me, music. Of course there were lots to choose from but it did not take long for me to gravitate toward those who sang from the heart. It was the voice and the words and the music that picked me up and carried me away. My room became the sanctuary that I so badly required and music, my medicine.

My father was gone, a harsh reality. I sat in the very chair where he had sat in weeks before, staring at the same screen that we all, as a family, enjoyed, but he was not there. But she was, the nice barefoot girl, sitting in a rocking chair, singing to me, "I'm just sittin' back sittin' here lovin' you." For a moment I felt better..........

I first realized that the voice that was singing was singing to me when I heard the words "I can't believe that you're honestly thinking of leaving me......." Well now that is exactly what I was wondering..."Until the light says goodbye to the night and your face I see, I'll just keep biding my time while the glow from the wine makes a fool of me......" ----- If I am a good boy and a good man then one day we will all be together again. There's that Catholicism again. Okay then tell me more.

......" it's a long distance phone and I feel so alone here without him...... it's a crime and a shame that I don't have the change and don't you know that I'm worried about him…" Then it was time to put a face to the words. Anne Murray was singing songs, sad songs…."Hard as I try I can't reach him…." I liked her voice and I could relate to the words. Not her words. Those were the very sad words of Gene MacLellan, Anne just made them bearable. So I kept listening and through the singing I found hope. "Put your hand in the hand of the man who stilled the water…" The sadness began to fade…."Got a feeling in my heart, that it's time for us to start to sing….sing together again" It was again through music that I could feel the darkness begin to fade. The worst two years of my life were coming to an end and I, Todd Canton was feeling better. Anne Murray, who was trying to find a place in the music business was making a significant impression in my heart. Her way was my way and I was hooked.

Over the years as I matured so did Anne's music and my attitude toward it. I am happy to say that I slow-danced to You Needed Me at my wedding and all of us have waltzed to and sang along with Could I have this Dance, even if you don't want to admit that you knew the words.

So now when I go to school everyday at junior high, and I look into the faces of those troubled individuals whom I work with, I see bits and pieces of my own life. I use, to the best of my ability, my life's lessons telling them that you really can overcome obstacles in your life, to never give up and that there is always 'hope'. I should know.

Forty years of music and a lifetime of memories that go with each and every tune. I wasn't the only one who thought Anne Murray was singing to them but I bet I was the one who appreciated it the most.

I told you it was personal……….

Remembering Rhonda

This year for Christmas my wife surprised me with a turntable that if hooked up to a laptop, allows you to put your records on CD. What a great gift for me as I have a great love for music and about three thousand records. Now I am able to hear my music in the car. On the table in my music room downstairs there lies a Tommy Makem,/Clancy Brothers album that I must get in the mail before January 25th, My friend Rhonda's birthday. She lives in Rhode Island and I am sure she will be totally surprised to receive it in the mail.

I first met Rhonda Mansfield in Springhill, Nova Scotia, standing in line at the Anne Murray Centre. She, like me and hundreds of others, was there to talk to and interact with our favorite singer. It was summer and it was hot. During our time in line together I struck up a conversation with her and the lady with her, Molly. They were American. Where are you from? I inquired, "Rhode Island", Rhonda said, "and Connecticut" was Molly's reply. Where are you from? They asked, "Truro" I said, knowing full well either of them would not have any idea where that was. "Oh", she said, "is your name Todd?" My eyeballs nearly popped out of my head. "You know who I am?" I asked, with a much puzzled expression in my voice and on my face. "I'm Rhonda, from the Snowbirds Internet site." At that moment our fate was sealed. I knew who Rhonda was, a knowledgeable person where "my" Anne was concerned. Up until that time I wasn't aware of fans that were as devoted as I was. She proved different. Suddenly it was "our" Anne, not just mine. It seems that Rhonda and Molly were seasoned pros where Anne was concerned and that the two of them traveled all over to see the star.

So as we talked, we bonded, I felt close enough to her and Molly to invite them to my home the next afternoon for a visit and for some seafood chowder. As it turned out, Rhonda was a seafood lover, and she felt enormously at home in the Maritimes. At one point during the conversation she told me she had plans to move up here, near Pugwash and build or buy a home of her own. Wow, I thought to my self, someone who appreciates the beauty of Nova Scotia as much as I do.

So what happened as a result of that visit and all those that followed was a deep and lasting friendship was forming. I was able to see through Rhonda's tough exterior and see for myself what a tender hearted soul she really was. Her sense of humour was a lot like my own and our interests, especially in music and movies was quite similar. When we disagreed I simply told her she was wrong.......actually, we agreed to disagree. I respected her for that. She was especially fond of my dog Rozie and my cat India, and Miss Bette Davis. Since she was an animal lover herself it just strengthened our bond. Rhonda's and my friendship grew over the next few years and we would speak on the phone at least once a month, talking sometimes, for hours. She was truly a friend in the fact that I could talk to her about anything and she did the same with me. We never wanted anything else. I always sent her my first draft of stories I had written and she would comment honestly. If she didn't like something, she told me, if she did, she told me that too. Her encouragement meant so much. In fact, I promised her that when my first book gets published (as if) I would dedicate it to her. I never thought I would do it posthumously.

My heart is broken in my grief because she and I were supposed to enter a new phase of our relationship, as neighbors. She was supposed to move up here, be within visiting distance, drop by for Sunday BBQ's, and continue our shared interest in Anne Murray. Now all I have is memories.

I knew Rhonda battled ill health over the years but she was so strong otherwise and determined that I guess I thought she would be around forever. So, when I opened my email on New Year's Eve I was shocked and saddened at the news. Stunned really!

But, what can I do, it's something we all face sooner or later and we are forced to accept it. I will say this. Of all of the people that I've met over the years, and there have been plenty, I was most impressed with you Rhonda.

I never made it a secret how much I cared for you, nor did I hide it from anyone else. Who knows why fate brought us together, not me, that's for sure but I do know that I am a better man for knowing you and a better person for loving you.

Sleep well my Snowbird, I love, I miss you. God Bless you!

Grieving

Today I am at home from work, sick, and it's one of those bugs where you only want to sleep. I feel miserable and I look green around the gills. In this state I quickly can become depressed. When something like that happens I pick up the phone. Usually I phone my sister Ruth either at home or work. She usually cheers me up but if I need a real punch in the arm I call my friend Rhonda Mansfield. She always puts me in the right frame of mind.

However, Rhonda passed away unexpectedly, just before we rang in the New Year and that really threw me for a loop. Rhonda was a constant in my life. She herself was a lot like me in her personality, strong and determined. We got along well. And we could talk about anything. She has a grown son, a dog, a sharp wit, a quick mind and even quicker eye. That's why, I suppose, she is such a fantastic photographer.

She battled ill health all of her adult life but I never thought it would get the best of her. She went in for a routine operation, slipped into a coma before hand and died while in there. I believe it must have been a blood clot and it took her life. It took a piece of mine as well. I have never been the same since. It has been a long winter for us here in Nova Scotia because the weather has been so very cold and there has been a lot of snow and freezing rain. That cooped up feeling doesn't work that well with me. So I reach out in whatever form I have around me, my writing, the computer, the phone.

When the news came that Rhonda was gone, it shocked me more than anything. She was 49 years old. That is not old by any means these days. In fact the older I get the younger it seems. I am of the thinking that too much is catered to young persons who have not experienced enough life to really appreciate it. The absence of God worries me about the future because so many people don't think before they act and as a result show no remorse. Drug abuse is making it's way through our society and that saddens me as well. Nobody seems to be thinking with a clear head. Whatever it is, I feel we need to rethink a few things and once we do it will all come around again. Hopefully.

So, where do I go from here?

Well, my mother would tell me to cheer up. To be grateful for all I have not what I have not. She would give me the old "what for" for going on about something of which I have no control and so I had better accept it as a part of life. That would have made me feel better. My sister Ruth would agree with me on all sorts of levels some of which never would occur to me until I sit down and think about it. That usually makes me feel better too. And then there's Rhonda. She would spare no time in telling me how stupid I am to waste my time on thinking about her when there is so much more out there that I should be concentrating on. That would get me thinking, why in the hell did I call her anyway? But, of course, she would be right as well.

Still, no one can tell me how I feel and no one can tell me how I should grieve because that ladies and gentlemen is the one thing I have to do on my own. Will I be ok? Sure. Will I get over all this? Yes, but not completely. Will I ever erase Rhonda from my heart on off my mind, why would I? Because, on these days when the sun ain't shining and the whole world is busy, I turn my thoughts to those, who over the years took me as I am, accepted me warts and all, and made me feel important along the way. Rhonda, that is where I leave you, today and always, in the midst of my thoughts and in the corner of my heart.

Within My Heart

People in general make assumptions based on their own life experiences and quite often are correct. In other cases they might be well off base. Why don't you decide for yourself...

Since my wife and I have no children of our own it has been assumed by those who do, that our pets have become our children. We have been accused of spoiling them beyond repair and due to something lacking in our lives, accept them as a decent replacement for kids. Perhaps they are right in such assumptions but allow me to explain myself. I love my dog! Let me say it again, I love my dog! She, Rozie is a comical, entertaining clown who worships the very ground I walk on. For the past few years she sits patiently waiting for me to come home from work everyday and gives me such a warm reception when I get here, that I quite often find myself hurrying home just to be near her. She sits at my feet, sleeps in my bed at my feet, takes me for walks, shares my snacks and loves me to pieces. Who, in their right mind could not love that?

There is something about a boy and his dog. At 40 years of age, I am about the biggest boy you will ever meet. I simply refuse to grow up and my dog will attest to that. She fills my heart with joy and love and makes me want to go to any length to protect her. I am smart enough to know that she won't be here forever but I also realize that these days we share are the important ones. Yesterday, a beautiful Nova Scotia summer afternoon, warm and sunny, I sat on my patio deck in a yard that my wife has painstakenly transformed into a flowery haven. We ate a marvelous summer meal and watched the dog chase a butterfly around the back yard. I couldn't help but appreciate my life. My wife and I both work, we have vehicles, a decent home that will someday be paid for and we have a dog. These are the days that fill my heart with love.

On the inside of our modest home we have four house-cats. They are my pets. Each one has their own personality, funny quirks and tastes. Some have some not so funny quirks and poor taste. However! On the wall in our living room hangs a framed black & white portrait of my cat India, a pitch black, green eyed vixen of amazing strength and determination. That girl, was not my pet for fourteen years, she was my daughter. I had never had a closer relationship with anyone, animal or not, than I did with that girl. She didn't sit at the top of the stairs barking and waging her tail when I came home. She didn't take me for walks or even chase butterflies. She simply owned me and that was that. She sat with me if it suited her, she slept in the bed with me if that was to her liking, not at my feet, on my chest. That was her place and she had sole rights to it. She was a determined and willful cat and I think that gave her the will to live to the ripe old age of fourteen despite the fact that she was diagnosed with feline leukemia at the age of four. She opened my eyes to the beauty that is all around me and made me appreciate the color black. She also made me aware that things don't last forever. A hard lesson but a realistic one.

It's been a year since India left me and not a day goes by that she doesn't cross this heart of mine. To tell you truth, I wish she didn't. I could use the break. The last year has been like every other one, I go through the motions, I go to work, I eat my dinner, I walk my dog. All in all I think I handled the whole situation well. I do appreciate my life and all it offers...... but......... every once in a while I glance up into that portrait and there within the walls of my heart, she sits quietly and without harm. A pet, oh no people, that's my daughter.

That's All I Ask

My bashful wife Sherry hates it when I write loving things about her, too bad, I can't help a heart that overflows with love.....

Cool winter mornings can be romantic. At least they are when they are shared with a loved one. My wife Sherry and I have taken advantage of this winter and all it's snow by taking daily walks through the wooded area up behind our home. The air is crisp and fresh, leaving us both energized and relaxed upon our return. The path is well traveled by dog walkers and pedestrians who, like the two of us, take advantage of the nature that surrounds us in our truly beautiful part of the world.

During our walks we talk and sometimes we don't say a word.. We spotted a fox once and it was gone as quickly as it came. Quite often there are deer and once in awhile you might spot a racoon or two. It is nice to see nature in it's own natural habitat.

As we walked along the road, the full moon from last night was still vivid in the sky. By moonlight my wife looked particularly beautiful. I always thought she was nice looking but today it was so much more special. I reached out and took her hand. Thinking to myself, I realized that I have been holding that hand for a very long time. I first took her hand as a boyfriend, then again as a husband. I held her hand over the loss of loved ones and for any other reason imaginable, and then in a moment of silence between us this morning, I took her hand to tell her, I love you still.

In fact, love plays a major role in our lives. I grew up in a loving household and brought that love inside of me where ever I go. Our pets have filled our home with love, and Sherry fills my heart with love. Had it not been for her being there all these years I cannot imagine where I would have ended up. Either on a Hollywood stage or in a cardboard box on the street. Who knows? I am aware of one thing. I am a better man for having met her. She added something valuable to my life without me realizing it right away. She brought faithful love and tenderness and in her own quiet way, embraced my heart for a lifetime.

Despite the hurdles we have faced over the years, we always seem to be closer rather than allowing anything to break us up. Love really is strong and it is constantly tested in life. She has had to put up with my clumsiness and awkward approach to life while she is so organized and meticulous. It just makes me want to do better.

It all comes down to one thing in the end. As we march forward in this world it is great comfort to me to have someone so wonderful at my side. I made a promise many years ago to put her first in my thoughts and actions and I believe I have done that. In return she has provided me with a private and comfortable personal life filled with laughter and music and food.. My final request, from those blue eyes to those soft and tender hands.........love me, that's all I ask of you.............

Winter Meeting

Our pastures were lightly covered with snow. That is always a good thing. It's December and this is the time for snow. Since global warming is upon us, I feel much better when we have seasonal and predictable weather when we are supposed to. It's easier on my pets too. The horses consume hay and are happy to be in the warmth of the barns. I enjoy the walk to the barns in the morning. So does my dog, Rozay. She is a collie mix and is the most faithful companion a man could ask for.

Moving to a farm was the smartest thing my wife and I have ever done. The horses aren't ours. We allow the neighbor to use the facilities at his own risk. I much prefer chickens and ducks, and the wild deer that feed on the perimeter of our property. I built the henhouse myself, I even assisted in building suitable quarters for our ducks alongside the pond in our back yard. It really makes it beautiful. As winter settles in the chickens stay inside and get plump. Not only do they supply us with fresh eggs but they are sometimes, our main course. I cannot kill a chicken myself and I refuse to eat duck. I am too tender-hearted to do the killing but I do enjoy eating part. That goes for the beef too. My neighbor John Morgan always fills our freezer with freshly cut roasts and we enjoy them thoroughly.

The reason I live on a farm is to lower my stress level. It was either that or die, my doctor informed me. So I listened. I love chickens and view them more as pets than I do a farm animal. I just want them taken care of. The ducks are for a selfish reason. I fell in love with waterfowl as a boy and since then, I simply enjoy watching them and listening to them chat the day away. They are in their own little world and I do my best to keep them safe from any predators.

Up behind the barns, my wife and I each have a garden. In the summer months I grow vegetables and she grows flowers. Both are beautiful and cultivated. Mine is fenced in so the wild deer and jack rabbits don't eat all I've grown, and she has carefully crafted a fence for all her colorful and pretty flowers to embrace.

After working in business for so long I didn't think I would like all the quiet but I have adapted nicely. The air is clean and fresh and so is our life out here. It's the walks I take around the wooded property that fascinates me the most. To see wildlife in it's natural habitat in whatever form, is heartwarming.

There is a tall, old, wooden fence that separates our acreage from our neighbors, and it stands strong. All along the fence the view is beautiful. Quite often in the Spring you will see a doe or two with a fawn. I thought the fence was to divide our properties, but later, I find out it was to keep the deer at a respectful distance. They really are beautiful creatures and as long as I knew the boundaries, I was able to view them without threat of interference on my part.

One doe in particular caught the scent of mine in the wind and that will usually cause the group to disperse. She seemed comfortable in my presence. Perhaps she had contact with man on a friendly basis over the course of time and felt unthreatened. I probably shouldn't do it but I often find myself bring carrot greens and apples to the fence and with my strongest arm, throwing them over. I know the deer enjoys this because I think they look for me. My newest friend, Sophie, comes the closest to the fence. She is like the lookout. Once she says it's okay, then it's a go for the rest.

There is something special about Sophie. She 's gentler than the others and more trusting too. This could be a dangerous thing for all of us. That's why I try to keep a respectful distance. She does come close enough that I can see how pretty her eyes are. Eyes are the mirror to the soul, isn't that what they say? She looks at me tenderly and sometimes tilts her head in amazement, the whole time on the alert for noises in front and back of her.

Yesterday she didn't show. In fact none of them walked along the fence wall. It was a reasonable day and for the life of me, I could not imagine what was going on. After a day or two things were back to normal. When I mentioned to John Morgan the mysterious events, he told me one of them must've given birth, and without Sophie, none would be allowed to leave the herd. All would form a circle around the doe and fawn until it was up and running. How magnificent I thought this was, a real miracle. John Morgan was right. There in the middle of the herd, a young doe had her fawn ever so near. Sophie, for the first time approached the fence. Standing inches from me, I could see her breath in the cool morning air, and had the chance to look into those beautiful eyes. From my hand I offered her a large carrot with a huge green top. Gently she took it from me and walked over and placed it at the feet of the young mother.

My heart was pounding so loud I could hear it in my ears. She really was the matriarch of the group. I think this little fawn was her grand-daughter and she brought them out to see me. I was never so humble in business as I was in the beauty of my own back yard.

Nature is wondrous, life is beautiful.

The Color of Coal

It seems that of all the stories that I have written about my beloved family, the Gillis's, I have certainly taken the time to glamorize their battles in life of the coal mine. I can't help it, I think that their's was a romantic and quite a desperate time. I love them all and I think that if I take the time to remember and acknowledge them, then I know that I would have made my mother proud, and GOD knows that's all I ever wanted to achieve as a human being on this Earth.

What I want to know as a human being is why did my people choose such a dirty and disgusting life like that of the dusty coal mines?. Was it the only jobs available? I realize that Springhill was not a rich town but were their no factories, mills, etc.? Death was surely imminent and yet so many of those men chose that life......for what in the end, I am at least allowed to ask.

Okay, so I talked about the men below the ground, and I talked about the women above the ground, and how both battled the coal mines in different and yet similar ways, and that there was always something to be lost.

Then it was brought to my attention that those who were chosen to work in the mines were the best at what they did. They were the true experts and who on earth wouldn't hire them? After all, it was a dirty job and some one had to do it, right? So, off they went, the Gillis's, the Rushton's and the Ruddick's and the rest of the hardworking gang that brought the much needed coal to the surface so we all could have warm and cozy homes, hot food on the stove and a worn and beaten father at our table. Who could ask for more? I did!

I am constantly amazed at the stories of resilience and tenacity where these very down to earth people were concerned. Not one's to carry any aires about themselves. They simply tackled the task at hand and did the job that needed to be done. I was proud to learn that giving up was not an option. You just kept going along, working, eating, living and dying. And for what I ask in the end, to leave a lonely widow and grieving children behind? Sad when one really thinks about it.

After being directly involved in a mine collapse or an explosion, or both, the way a coal mining man

thinks begins to change. His outlook on life is included in this change, and he leans closer to God more than ever. This man, whether he be black or white, gentile or jew, knows no color in the mine. They are all, after all, human beings.

So then one day, a gentle father looks across his dinner table to his lovely wife and into the faces of his children, and he sees something that he never noticed before. Innocence. He comes to the realization that throughout his whole hardworking life, he just seemed to get old before his time. Did he want the same for his sons? Did he want his daughters to marry men who were tired and sick at the end of the workweek? There had to be a better life out there. So with a little encouragement on his part, the idea was planted that it was a big world out there and maybe they should be given the chance to see some of it.

That is how Dan Gillis felt about his daughter Vivian, how Angus Gillis felt about his kids Sam and Vivian, I am sure that how Maurice Ruddick felt about his kids. There had to be a better life for our children and their children.

When the Springhill Mine Explosion happened in 1956 and the bump in 1958, the whole world watched to see the outcome. They were introduced to the gentle people of Springhill and to the sense of community spirit that existed there. When the final group of men were brought to the surface, there they were, black faced, broken and beaten men. Each received their own bit of fame and attention from their part in the disaster . Songs were written about them, stories told, and legends were born. But, when the coal dust was wiped away and the bruises and cuts were healed, they, those brave men, those brothers in time of tragedy, were forced to resume their social roles. The blacks went back to their own poor community and the whites and others, to their's. Life above ground has always had it's upside and downs, but life goes on and as we all heal from the damage done to our families from the mine disasters, let us not ever forget these brave and valiant men, who from *all* communities, worked so hard to bring the valuable coal home to us, their families.

A Springhill Christmas

The year our sister Anne was born was a rough year on our family. As the story goes, our mother suffered distress in giving birth, putting both their lives at risk. When it came time to make a decision whether to save the mother's or the baby's life, there was no doubt in our mother's mind. "Save my child," she said, "My husband is a good man, he'll marry again." Our father on the other hand, said to save his wife. "I cannot raise six children alone." As it turned out, both of them made it. The doctor was firm that this was to be the last child. He told our mother this and she, well she disagreed. "I am Catholic," she stated emphatically, "I will have as many babies as God sees fit."

The doctor shook his head. As fate would have it, less than a year later, our sister Ruth was born. Both of these girls arrived by caesarean section. Since there was so much difficulty in their arrivals, I think it brought our mother closer to them. Once, someone asked our mother, who is your favorite child? To which she quickly replied," the one who needs me the most at the time."

So with a house that full, our mother needed a little assistance in getting Christmas under way. Mother's health had not been the greatest that year and to top it off, she caught the flu. So did Dad. He spent most of Christmas in the upstairs bedroom with the door closed and she, too weak to move about, found comfort in the downstairs bedroom, just off the kitchen. She lived on tea and toast.

There was no other choice but to ask for help. Enter **Nan**. There she was, a five foot tall, plump and feisty woman, all set and ready to go. **Francess Ann Gillis** at seventy years of age had the energy of a twenty year old. Her attitude toward life was that if there was work to do, then let's get at it. She was a spinster aunt to our mother who played a significant role in her raising. As far as that goes she played that role in the lives of all the people in house. After her parents passed on it was Nan that fed all the hungry coal miners, and there were lots of them too.

As a result she commanded respect and got it. I feel it is safe to say that she was a firecracker. Her quick wit was something to be admired. If she had been born into another family, at another time, I believe she would have eventually found her way to a Hollywood screen. Her pitch black hair was rolled up into a tight bun on the back of her head. The pins defied one strand of hair from leaving it's clutch.. Her matronly aprons embraced her strong body. Strong body and mind. She was a force to be reckoned with. Taking control was what she was best at.

She didn't like the turkey Mom bought for Christmas dinner so she brought her own. I can still see my brother Jack coming down the path behind Nan, carrying a twenty pound turkey. They had marched home from Goodwin's Supermarket. It was not long before the masterful chef had the turkey stuffed and sewn. Into the coal stove's oven it went. Then the potatoes had to be peeled. Not by her, by us. Like a drill Sargent she watched over each and every one of us. Carrots to dice, onions too. She liked to tell people what to do. Jack didn't like to peel onions so she made Susan do it. In fact, she made Susan do a lot. Probably because she rolled her eyes when Nan asked her to do something.

She took one look at Joan standing there in the kitchen and said "Instead of standing there like an oil painting, go and find the center for the table." Joan didn't like it but she didn't roll her eyes either. While the rest of us worked, Jack was allowed to go to the store, that's when Susan remarked that Nan played favorites. "Sure do" she said "Wanna be my favorite? Then peel some potatoes." Susan just rolled her eyes.

Mom always made dressing, not stuffing. Do you know the difference? One is mostly potato and the other is mostly bread. What Nan made was a masterpiece. To this day I compare turkey dressing to her's. So then it was time to set the table. It looked nicer than normal or maybe I was noticing it for the first time. I can say this though, it was a feast. The gravy wasn't lumpy, the turkey was moist and the cranberries were tart. And last but not least, sliced fruitcake from Mary Soppa. Beautiful. "There" she said with a big smile, "I brought you a Springhill Christmas."

Poor Dad! We didn't see him for days. Nan made Mom a special chicken soup from the broth with lots of barley and pepper. She always put pepper on everything. Mom sat up in bed looking a little green around the gills but you could tell she was feeling better. That's when Susan closed the door to Mom's sick room and told her that Nan had to go. Mom laughed. From the kitchen Nan bellowed "S U S A N, time for dishes". Susan rolled her eyes.

After ten days she decided she had had enough of us, so she called a taxi to take her to the bus terminal. When she turned to our mother in the kitchen she looked her in the face and said "Thanks for having me, it's nice to be needed." "Now get yourself some rest and keep warm." Before she closed the door, she hollered one more time "S U S A N, there are floors to be scrubbed." No one had to be in the room with Susan to know she rolled her eyes.

Out the door she went, home to Springhill where she took a piece of our hearts with her.

This is her story. When you are raised in a Catholic coal mining family around the turn of the century, you marry a Catholic. The man Francess Gillis fell in love with was Protestant. She couldn't get him off her mind or out of her heart. Unmarried and pregnant, her fate was sealed. Spinster. No man wanted a sullied woman. Old fashioned by today's standards, it was what it was. So the girl named Sarah was born into the fold. Nan insisted on a bigger and better life for "Sadie" as she was known to us. That life took her first to Toronto and then to LA. A far cry from the dreary town of Springhill, Nova Scotia. Sadie had kids of her own but her visits became less and less frequent. Nan would never say if anything ever bothered her. What we liked about her was the fact that she thought so much of our mother. She may have raised her but we weren't allowed to call her our grandmother. Everyone called her Nan. She never looked at another man in all the years that followed. Nan lived out the rest of her days with her brother's widow and family, making life for all, trying at times. She died at 84 years of age from heart complications brought on by diabetes. *Don't know how Susan felt about her but I loved her very much!*

Shelly Gee, I am Sorry!

A long time ago, perhaps longer than I am willing to remember, I made a horrible mistake. I think we all did. You do know what I mean, don't you?

Living in, and growing up with the snotty people I did, in the town of Amherst, was to say the least, challenging. I wasn't an athlete, I wasn't a scholar, and I wasn't a millionaire. I was just a poor boy from the wrong side of the tracks.

My father died when I was in grade six and that left an empty void in my life. Even though I grew up in a picturesque neighborhood, I survived despite my short-comings. Like most teens, I was emotionally wrapped up in my distaste for life. My best friend was Brian Ripley, my closest friend was another Brian, an adopted boy. I so envied his hockey skills, his popularity, and his having any other family but his own. My emotions and loneliness may have run a bit deeper than his did but still I envied him, he had an escape. He had another mysterious family somewhere.

I was forced against my will to attend senior high, otherwise known as Amherst Regional High School. I hated every moment of it! Okay, there were a few bright moments, the way Mrs. Pipes made me feel and then there was Mr. Angel and his choice of songs for the music class, but there was little else.

I did not like school, I did not like the long walk to school, and I did not like having to force myself into entering the building on any level. Those were really not my people. Get it?

It was a building full of misfits, jocks, dead-heads, druggies, losers and me. How we all survived, I will never know. It probably due to the fact that I met decent friends like Brian, Duncan and Kevin that got me through the rough times.

And then it is a coming of age moment for me, a truly eye opening experience. A crazy girl from just outside of town, someone who today might have been diagnosed as bi-polar, was picked on, no I should say, she was harassed, or should I say, she was targeted. Shelly G. was a nervous and emotional girl who, looking back now, was kicked while she was down. It got to the point that she was crying every day. I never cried, so I had no sympathy for someone so emotionally unstable. Kids pounced on her weakness. She was harassed in the halls and picked on in the stairwell, so much so, that one evil day someone pulled her by the book bag and caused her to fall down the stairs backwards, head over heels. I saw her lying at the bottom of the stairs, crying.

It occurred to me than that I was the worst one there. Oh, I wasn't the one who caused that girl to fall, I was the one who said nothing. I did nothing. That made me the worst of all. To this day that very act of cruelty has haunted me. I was the one that did not speak up, I was the one that allowed another human being to be treated like dirt and for what, so someone who had more going for them than she did, would feel superior to her, and to us, and to the world? I think not!

Shelly G., wherever you are, take my word as a man, from this day forward, I, Todd Canton, stand up for those individuals who, for whatever reason, decide to prove themselves different, so that every child, no matter who they are, or where they come from, that they all, and I mean all, have the chance to experience high school in a safe and friendly environment with at least one individual who will speak up when I see an injustice, and because of you, I am not afraid to do so.

God Bless you wherever you are.

Epilouge: Another Pot o' Tea

It is a ritual in our family to put on a pot of tea when someone arrives to visit. In our family coffee is saved for the drive to work in the mornings. Tea, on the other hand, fits in with every celebration.

Our mother used to steep tea on the coal stove in her kitchen but we do it a cup at a time, mostly because we all like it at different strengths. Our sister Susan cools her's down with a drop of cold water, while I like mine steaming hot, the stronger the better. However we enjoy it, it is symbolic that we all enjoy being together.

Spending time with my family is something I do not do very often. The winter keeps us apart the most. My busy schedule keeps me just that, busy. I work every weekend of the year so that doesn't give me a lot of time to do anything. Like family reunions and such. It's sad but true. I like to keep busy, it keeps my mind occupied.

My sisters Anne and Ruth are the ones who do the most interacting with our family. Their's is the house where everyone gathers and it is the centerpiece of our lives. It is the home they shared with and took care of, our mother. For that we are all grateful, for that we are all glad. Missing our mother is something we all do in different ways, not unlike our cups of tea. Some don't talk very much about it and others speak of her as if she was in the other room. Whatever works.

However one chooses to remember our mother is up to the individual. I think we can all agree on the following. Our fondest memories are most often at our home on Russell Street in Amherst, where she was quite often sitting in a chair reading Redbook Magazine or a Harlequin romance.

The curtains tossing in the breeze because our windows were often open so the marsh winds would infiltrate our home and mix with the smell of Red Rose tea steeping, it invited us inside to where she was, our lovely and entertaining mother, whose thoughts were all so full of us. It seemed she lived each day for her children and we, in return would run home to her, to share with her, the events of our day.

These are the memories I carry in my heart on the days I think I can go on no longer or I feel like giving up. She would tell me not to be discouraged as there is so much more out there to see, food to taste, people to meet and nature to explore. And there is............so as I march forward in this life, I carry with me a lifetime of memories, good and bad, with one thought in mind............put on another pot o' tea, I'll soon be home.

Thank you all for taking a journey down memory lane to my childhood, my family and of course, my mother. Take care and be well.

Richard Todd Canton